Contents

Introduction

There's a story about a factory, somewhere in the United States, that had a problem. A distressingly large percentage of employees became accident-prone at five in the afternoon. As soon as it was time to leave, everybody rushed down the one stairway to their cars. The headlong impatience caused a number of bruises, twisted ankles, broken wrists, and other damage to anatomy.

The resulting absences was a concern. Employers tried different solutions that turned out to be unpersuasive. Signs were displayed urging people to slow down. Statements about safety were made over loudspeakers. Hired voices pleaded and preached until everyone was sick of it.

Nothing worked. People still hurtled themselves pell-mell down the stairs. Bones kept breaking.

Then one young person came up with the right idea: he placed a full-length mirror on the landing. From then on, everybody just naturally slowed down to take a look at themselves. The new approach was a subjective attention-getter. "Personal sense," it seems, is more appealing than "common sense."

This book of stories tries to provide the same service as that mirror on the landing of the stairs. It is easy to rush through the words of the Gospel. We are so familiar with certain favorite parts and we limit ourselves to these. There are other less famous passages that can serve as reflectors for self-understanding, and as launchers for Christ-directed prayer.

These chapters tell the stories of a number of individuals who made some kind of contact with Jesus during his three-year public ministry. Each of them comes on the scene, does something significant...and is never mentioned again. They make one cameo appearance and then drop out of sight. The person is never named.

Whatever it was that they said and did has been remembered for two thousand years. But our recognition of them as this or that person is usually a superficial one. They are passing acquaintances whose names have escaped us. They are the kind of persons we would refer to as "What's-his-name" or "What's-her-name." Jesus himself called one of these individuals "so-and-so." (See Chapter 2.) Their deeds can be brought to mind. Some of their responses have actually become catch-phrases. But the character-sketch of any of them in the Gospels has been a bit too sketchy to leave any lasting impression.

Because of their anonymity, they make it all the easier for us to identify with them. (For further explanation of this book's method of identifying Gospel people to ourselves, see the Appendix.) They are ordinary people, like ourselves. They figured personally, rather than prominently, in the mission of Jesus. Their stories can become our own...as soon as we slow down long enough to see ourselves in them, as in a mirror.

Some of these pages are simply restatements of what the Evangelists already have said. The others are my elaborations. I have made some guesses about the character, and character traits, of people who have said very little for themselves. What I have written "para-scripturally" has been taken from clues contained in the Gospel text itself and from my understanding of other ordinary people, including myself.

I have ruminated on, and prayed about, these fascinating individuals. Little by little, they came to life for me. They became mirrors by which I saw myself responding to Jesus and being taught by him. It seemed as though our Lord was looking through What's-his-name or What's-her-name and speaking directly to me.

Perhaps this book can do the same for you. Perhaps you can let these unnamed Gospel people show you to yourself. You can pause in your rush of living and slow down long enough to see them as you would see a fascinating mirror that has just now been placed on the landing of your stairs.

1

The Barley Boy

Looking up, Jesus saw the crowds approaching and said to Philip, "Where can we buy some bread for these people to eat?" He only said this to test Philip; he himself knew exactly what he was going to do. Philip answered, "Two hundred denarii would only buy enough to give them a small piece each."

One of his disciples, Andrew, Simon Peter's brother, said, "There is a small boy here with five barley loaves and two fish; but what is that between so many?"

Jesus said to them, "Make the people sit down." There was plenty of grass there, and as many as five thousand men sat down. Then Jesus took the loaves, gave thanks, and gave them out to all who were sitting ready; he then did the same with the fish, giving out as much as was wanted.

When they had eaten enough, he said to the disciples, "Pick up the pieces left over, so that nothing gets wasted." So they picked them up, and filled twelve hampers with scraps left over from the meal of five barley loaves.

The people, seeing this sign that he had given, said, "This really is the prophet who is to come into the world."

John 6:1-14; Matthew 14:13-21;
Mark 6:31-44; 8:1-9; Luke 9:10-17

We don't know his name. He only appears once in the Gospels. He does one simple thing or to be more accurate, he lets something be done to him. He gives something up. He lets the Apostle Andrew take something precious from him with, doubtless, no more than a simple "thank you" in return.

Since he has no name, let us call him "The Barley Boy." Five barley loaves are more closely connected with his character than the two fish; besides, it's a more appealing name than "The Fishy Fellow" or something like that.

His deed (and his "letting-be-done") is a beautiful example of what could be called "NBDBP Christianity" — No Big Deal, But Practical.

In a sense, it was no big deal. Andrew himself said as much. "There is a boy here with five barley loaves and two fish; but what are these among so many?" The contents of his knapsack (or was it his pushcart?) could hardly have satisfied the appetite of two people. There were thousands more making up the "many."

No big deal perhaps, but it was a kind and generous thing he did. He could have been selfish. He could have been a shrewd opportunist. Hunger was happening; the demand was getting great and the supply was very low. To put it in terms of supply and demand, the boy could have sold his barley loaves for $5.99 a crumb! He could have made a bundle.

He didn't. Andrew returned to him and said, "The Master has need of your food," or something to that effect. And that's the last we see of the Barley Boy.

Apparently, it was a brief exchange. Everything in St. John's Gospel indicates that the boy, like Mary, simply said, "O.K., let it be done to me according to his wishes." Doubtless, he stayed around to see what Jesus would do with his provisions. Of course, he was as awestruck as the others, maybe more so, for he knew the whole sequence of events that started with his modest gift of unselfish generosity.

No big deal, but very practical. With this meagre picnic lunch for two, Jesus fed thousands to their satisfaction and had bushelsful to spare. Jesus used a human "little bit of kindness" and magnified it to unheard-of generosity.

And more than this: Jesus showed us in a way not to be denied how compassionate he is. St. Mark's Gospel mentions the reason for his feeding the multitude: "I feel sorry for all these people; they have been with me for three days now and have nothing to eat. If I send them home hungry, they will collapse on the way" (Mark 8:2-3).

Jesus does not want us to "faint on life's journey;" he wants us to be renewed with the nourishment which only he can give (using our "little bit of kindness").

And even more: thanks to the few-rolls-become-a-feast, Jesus can be remembered, rightly, for the gift of himself in the Sacrament of Bread. The Body of Christ which we receive at Holy Communion is not a gold medal declaring we are in the state of grace. It is food — Jesus giving himself as food — Heavenly Bread given for the same purpose that the barley bread was given centuries ago: so that we do not collapse on our journey, so that we do not grow weary or give up because of fear, anxiety, or discouragement.

The Barley Boy had good reason to be proud of himself. He had to be happy about the way God worked this sign of compassion. Jesus demonstrated his Father's kindness, thanks to this No-Big-Deal-But-Practical little bit of barley thoughtfully given by an unnamed person, who is simply called "a boy who happened to be there."

We all possess that same quality. One way or another, we have a bit of the Barley Boy within ourselves. More often than not, especially in those actions that are spontaneous, we are more kind than unkind, more caring than selfish.

Most of this activity is in the NBDBP category. What we do are little things . . . nothing extraordinary: a visit to the sick; a phone call to the lonely; encouragement to the depressed; grocery shopping or sidewalk shovelling for those who can't get around so well; a hand of friendship for those who feel they don't belong; a hand of applause for those who need the hospitality of our appreciation; food for the hungry (which could simply mean pleasant meals at home); drink for the thirsty (which could simply mean a smile or a kind word for those who thirst for just this much to get them through the day); and all the things by which we get our blessings in the next life (Matthew 25:31-40) and through which Jesus can continue to give his kindly love in the present life, in the world we know around us.

No big deal, perhaps. But when the thoughtfulness is practical, and especially when it is done so that others will not falter on their journey through discouragement or fear, it stirs up thoughtfulness in others. It is the raw material by which Jesus can make himself understood as the "Nourisher of the many."

There are two obstacles that will hinder the "Barley Boy within us" from taking its rightful place as part of our personality. One obstacle is obvious. The spirit of "No Big Deal, But Practical Christianity" can be blocked by selfishness, by operating with our version of selling barley loaves at $5.99 per crumb and gaining personal profit from other people's needs.

Most of the acts of selfishness come in our brooding moments, when self-pity magnifies "all I've done for others" and then whimpers back at itself: "And see how they use me" . . . or "take me for granted" . . . or "don't give me back nearly as much as I give them!" In such a mood, the "Barley Boy within" can be murdered. The mood can pronounce the death sentence on all further acts of kindness: "If that's the way life is . . . if that's the way they want it . . . okay . . . I'll look out for 'Number One' from now on . . . I'll give of myself, my deeds, my words, yes, even of my gestures and my smiles, but only when I get something out of it for myself!"

This is one obstacle to watch out for. The other one is not so obvious, but just as dangerous. It could be called "Thoughtlessness about our thoughtfulness." Because so much of our kind deeds are such little things — with "No Big Deal" written all over them — we tend to dismiss them as soon as they happen. Whenever we do take note of them, it is very often a long time afterward; then they are magnified all out of proportion in order to feed our mood of self-pity mentioned above.

It would be better if we relished our capacity for kindness and enjoyed — easily and gracefully — the good effects that have happened because of our kindness. This will not cause us to be proud. After all, what we have done was "no big deal." Our little bit has meant much to someone who was helped by it. This will encourage us to do more of the same, and do other kindnesses we had not thought about before, and do them with a better understanding of why we do them — linking our little acts of consideration with the large caring ways of Christ who loves us so much that he gives us the nourishment of himself so that we do not get weary or grow faint along the way.

Prayer of the Barley Boy Within

Jesus, my Lord,
Please give me more of the spirit of the Barley Boy.
I do not know whether you thanked him, personally,
    for his barley loaves and fishes.
Perhaps you nodded his way as you said those words
    that meant compassion on the many;
Perhaps you smiled so that he saw that you gave thanks to him,
    as well as to your Father;
Perhaps you had some time to speak to him in private,
    thanking him in your own words,
    while your disciples were collecting all the leftovers . . .
I don't know.
I do know he could see that his little gift of kindness
    was taken up by you and made into magnificence.

Let me understand my ways of kindness this way.
I sometimes feel unnamed like that boy in your Gospel
    — unnoticed, anyway.
The people of my world, so often, have so many needs,
    so much discouragement and sickness,
    such weariness,
    so many reasons to give up.
What good, I wonder sometimes, is the little bit
    that I can do for them?

And also, I don't see your smile, your word of thanks
    for my version of the gifts of barley loaves and fishes.
I have to simply know, by faith,
    that your great love
    is something like my little loving deeds.
And your huge acts of mercy can somehow be understood
    a little better
    when I, and others, act in kindly ways.

Help me to be more thoughtful of my thoughtfulness.
Make sure I don't compare my deeds
    — which are, really, no big deal —
    in such a fashion that I begin to think
    I give more than I get in life.

I have a certain number of gifts,
    a certain group of friends and family,
    a certain range of possibilities for good,
    opportunities for kindness.
These are my barley loaves and fishes.
Let me give them as the gifts of my practical Christianity.

And let me, thanks to these,
    rejoice more fully
    in your greater gift of nourishment to me.

Amen.

2

Mr. Gobetween

Now on the first day of Unleavened Bread, the disciples came to Jesus to say, "Where do you want us to make the preparations for you to eat the passover?"

He replied, "Go to so-and-so in the city and say to him, 'The Master says: My time is near. It is at your house that I am keeping Passover with my disciples'."

The disciples did what Jesus told them and prepared the Passover.

Matthew 26:17-19

The day of Unleavened Bread came round, the day on which the Passover had to be sacrificed, and he sent Peter and John saying, "Go and make the preparations for us to eat the Passover."

"Where do you want us to prepare it?" they asked.

He said to them, "Go into the city and you will meet a man carrying a pitcher of water. Follow him, and say to the owner of the house which he enters, 'The Master says: Where is my dining room in which I can eat the Passover with my disciples?'

"He will show you a large upper room furnished with couches, all prepared. Make the preparations for us there."

The disciples set out and went to the city and found everything as he had told them . . .

Mark 14:12-16; Luke 22:7-13

*T*he accommodating host of the Last Supper is one of the most generous and unselfish persons recorded in any history. His untold story is one of the most beautiful ever hinted at.

The Gospels skip over his significance. All we can do is imagine the personality of this man who was deliberately left unnamed. We can only conjure him up from clues that are vague almost to the point of a conspiracy of silence.

As far as the Evangelists are concerned (and, apparently, Jesus too) all the preparations for the Last Supper were very much hush hush. In St. Matthew's account, there is no question that the planning for this great event was a very private affair. Jesus definitely withheld the name of his benefactor. "Where do you want us to make preparations for the Passover?" the disciples asked. Obviously, they were unadvised about any preliminary arrangement. Jesus had done this all on his own. Our Lord replied, "Go to so-and-so. He is in the city. Say to him, 'The Master says: My time is near; it is at your house that I am keeping Passover with my disciples'."

St. Matthew concludes with the brief statement: "The disciples did what Jesus told them and prepared the Passover."

That's it; that's all there is. It is the last thing mentioned, or even suggested, about the unnamed man who so graciously opened his house and provided a lavish meal, in a quiet setting, for thirteen people.

Jesus even called him "so and so." No name. Such a designation was not a put-down, of course. But it was an evasion. It was as if Jesus said, "Never mind who he is, or what his name is. That is between the two of us. Too many important things will be taking place tonight to let such incidental matters get in the way."

Two other Gospels provide a detail which shows that at least the disciples didn't have to go on a wild goose chase. Saint Luke states that Jesus sent his two favorite disciples, Peter and John, on this important errand. Both Mark and Luke remember what their precise instructions were. Jesus told them: "You will meet a *man* carrying a pitcher of water. Follow him and say to the owner of the house which he enters: 'The Master says: Where is *my* dining room in which I can eat the Passover with my disciples?' He will show you a *large* upper room, *furnished* with couches, all *prepared*..."

I emphasize the most fascinating words. 1. Peter and John need not run about the city wildly calling out for someone who fitted the vague description of "so and so." A *man* doing a woman's job of carrying water from the well would be a dead giveaway. For that time and culture, it was very bizarre behavior. His master must have been extremely persuasive to get him to do something that would make him the laughing-stock of the town. Actually, the master would be made a laughing-stock as well. It was he who subjected his servant to such humiliation. Only women carried water. Such a task would make a man feel that he was almost emasculated.

2. Peter and John went off on their pursuit. They had no trouble picking out this weird character from the crowd. They must have been surprised, however, by our Lord's unaccountable use of the possessive pronoun *my*. Everything seems to have been secretly arranged. Jesus already understood that a large part of so-and-so's house was "*my* dining room."

3. Added to all this, the room was not only *large*; it was *well furnished* with the best accommodations and everything was already prepared. Grocery shopping was done; cooks were getting things in order; servants were thoroughly instructed on how to serve the meal and when to leave the guests alone.

We'll never know who this private person was. Everything in the Gospel indicates that we aren't supposed to know. We can assume a number of things with reasonable confidence. The man was fairly wealthy. Not everybody has the wherewithal to welcome thirteen guests into his home and guarantee that they will be undisturbed. The man had to be a friend of Jesus. Everything indicates that our Lord put in his reservation early. No one else was apprised of the plan beforehand. Somewhere, sometime, Jesus and friend spent a quiet afternoon stipulating what was needed and agreeing on all the right procedures, even to the detail about the servant doing a maid's chore.

Chances are, he was not a disciple. The Evangelists are very careful to designate those who distinguished themselves in the core group of the early Church. His task, apparently, was this one-shot operation. He was to be a benefactor of one particular function. Because of so many significant events that would take place that night — the institution of the Eucharist; the ordination of Christ's first priests; the reception of their first Holy Communion; the Last Will and Testament of him who was about to die; the awesome revelation of the New Covenant made in blood; the imperious demand that all Christ's followers must continue to "do this in memory of me" — because of all these solemn importances, the man who provided the logistics was pushed into the background. He was simply, and it seems deliberately, overlooked.

I do not want to go against our Lord's obvious intent. I have given him a simple generic name: "Mr. Gobetween." That is all he did; that is all he was, the necessary link that made it possible for the Last Supper to take place privately and leisurely.

No one knows what happened to him afterward. No one knows what happened to him even on that splendid night. I imagine he remained somewhere in the background. He must have been more than mildly interested. The Passover was a very solemn celebration anyway. Added to its usual importance was the special nature of this particular one. Jesus deliberately made it special by engineering all the secret preparations, which even his closest friends were in the dark about, by heightening their curiosity with those "cloak and dagger" arrangements that ushered in the eventful night, and by his own serious demeanor when he was shown the upper room and assured that all was ready.

The man must have been anxious to find out what in the world was going on behind closed doors. He probably would have given anything to have been a part of it. He wasn't. All the Gospels presume that except for the first courses of the meal served by the catering staff Jesus was left entirely alone with his chosen Twelve.

I visualize the man acting as a "go between" to the very end of the evening. He probably remained on the first floor, at the foot of the stairs, acting as a kind of bouncer, making sure that neither servants nor strangers ventured in to the proceedings of the upper room.

Perhaps Jesus thanked the man for his generous hospitality, as he put on his seamless garment to make his way with his stunned Apostles to the Garden of Gethsemane. Perhaps there were some private words at the end of the supper which were as comforting as they could be.

Perhaps there were no words at all. It may have been that Jesus was too preoccupied by what he had just done and said, and by what he would be facing later that night and the next day. His mind and heart were already too full to remember normal protocol.

We do not know. Neither Jesus nor the Evangelists seem to think it makes any difference, one way or the other. Unlike so many people in the Gospels who were praised for their faith or generosity, our Lord seems to think it either untimely or unnecessary to point out this man's notable qualities.

Jesus asked the two blind beggars (Chapter 8): "What do you want me to do for you?" He had asked many other people the same thing. With this man, the dialogue was reversed. Jesus said (during that preliminary planning session which the two had secretly engaged in): "I want you to do me a favor." The man must have replied: "What do you want me to do for you?" Jesus told him. At great sacrifice to himself, he readily agreed.

Mr. Gobetween did not need public praise. He was content to remain "in the wings." He was the chosen stage manager for the greatest drama the world has ever witnessed. He was the link between need and nourishment. He was the liaison between God's love for us and our ability, at last, to understand what this love really means.

All the individuals in this book present a personal challenge for my own development. The prayers at the end of each story are autobiographical; they are first mine, and then they belong to others. How can I feel that these Gospel people have a message for anyone else unless they first of all have a message for me?

As a priest for almost twenty years, much or even most of my ministry has been go-between. In the confessional, in counseling, in guided meditations, and in many other ways, my role is like that of the host at the Last Supper. I simply set the stage for God's love to take place. I "arrange the furniture" and set up suitable accommodations for a Christ-to-Christian rendezvous. I make sure there is space and leisure time so that Jesus may speak privately to the individual in whatever way he wishes. I am really left in the dark about what takes place in the upper chambers of someone else's prayer. This is a private and intimate time of grace; I was only the liaison between other people and our Lord.

I often get curious, however. It's none of my business, I know, but I often want to eavesdrop on divine proceedings. I want to know whether my humble preparatory work does any lasting good. I wonder whether anyone ends up unfaithful even after all my efforts? Which ones are like the Apostles who at Gethsemane fell asleep on our Lord...then ran away...and finally returned, after so many vicissitudes, to become friends Jesus could truly be proud of? "Is there any way to speed up God's process?" I ask myself. "Perhaps I should barge into the private meeting so that it would be more efficient for all concerned!"

In a word, I am tempted to forego my simple role of go-between and "play God" with the people Jesus has sent my way. I must remember Jesus just wants me to make the hospitable arrangements for *his* encounter. I need to pray for the good graces of the man in the Gospels who was only alluded to.

Often, both personally and in my calling as a priest, Jesus asks me to serve his purposes. I'd better not be too busy and refuse...or too much of a busybody to get in the way of his engagements. I'd better say, "What do you want me to do for you, Lord?" And even though some of it seems silly (like sending out a manservant to draw water); and even though it means a sacrifice of time and energy (like furnishing an upper room instead of enjoying it myself)...I'd better do it, and do it as generously as I can.

Jesus does not have just one Last Supper, in one upper room. He is not finished with his love; he has not concluded all further instructions to his friends. Whenever he wants to continue these upper-room-deliberations, I must continue in the spirit of Mr. Gobetween and take my place backstage — after I've made all the necessary arrangements.

Everyone needs this spirit. Opportunities to be a go-between are evident in all the helping professions: teachers, people in social services, doctors, nurses, politicians, counsellors of all kinds. Their task is to be a link of love and growth for other people. They do not give life — they facilitate the process that comes from within the people they serve. They are "arrangers of accessibility."

Tax money must be funneled honestly to help the people who are supposed to benefit by it. Nurses and those in social services should perform their tasks humbly — as the host of the Last Supper did — not bureaucratically (as though they were doing other people a great favor) or busybodily (as though the whole effectiveness of other people's success depended on their personal intervention). All the helping professions need the spirit of the one Jesus simply called "so and so." We need his agreeable generosity and his self-effacing willingness to do only what he was supposed to do.

Parents need it, too. It is difficult for parents to keep the good balance between caring enough to provide their children with a good atmosphere for growth and not caring so much that they try to butt in on God's patience or take Christ's place as the engineer of their children's version of "upper room encountering."

Everyone, one way or another, has many opportunities to be a go-between for the sake of others. It could be serving as a peacemaker between friends, a reconciler of bitterness between spouses or families, a mediator between gangs or neighborhoods or nations where there is racial tension or the threat of war. It could be introducing a stranger to a social club, or a new job, or an old friend. Often enough on these occasions, we who initiate the proceedings play only the role of "stage manager" while the real drama goes on without us. We are left in the dark, marginal to the real action.

It is difficult to meet the dual demands of enthusiasm about possibilities for new life and detachment about the results of these possibilities. We can either lose interest and get cynical ("Who is showing accommodation for the accommodator?") or else we can make a nuisance of ourselves by snooping into encounters that have no further need of our assistance.

We need the restraint, as well as the generosity, of the unnamed man who hosted the Last Supper. Who cares if we are left in relative anonymity? Who cares that we do not know exactly how things developed after we began the process of grace, or growth, or learning? It was a good thing to do. It seemed, somehow, that we were the ones to do it. We did it. We don't have to be praised for it. It is enough for us, as it was for the original Gobetween, to know that something good has happened to other people...and we had a hand in helping it to happen.

Prayer of Mr. Gobetween Within

Jesus, my Lord,
First, let me ask you to be kind
    to all those people who were go-betweens for me.
So many people helped me to know you better.
Some I remember well;
yet there are many others
    whose names I've lost
    as easily as the Evangelists
    left out the name of the Last Supper caterer.
They have been kind to me.
They gave me room to move toward you with love.
They gave me time to grow,
    with freedom to do it at the pace I needed.
They were accommodators to the best within me.
Most of them I forgot to thank or praise;
You do it for me, Lord,
    when you meet them again, in secret.

And do it for me, in secret,
    when I have go-between responsibilities.
Let me not lag,
    or carry on complainingly,
    when your grace suggests
    that I could be a link of love
    between you and another person;

or that I could be the means of reconciliation,
or an arranger for new learning to take place.
Let me agree to do all that I can
so that it may run smoothly.
Let me not linger, overlong,
into whatever happens afterward.
Sometimes it's right for me to stay with people
who, by my means, were touched with life and love.
Sometimes it's right to simply be the link
and let it go at that.
Help me to know which is which,
and to behave accordingly.

Above all, let me not seek praise
for the accommodating good I do.
Let me be like the man you didn't name
when I provide my versions of the upper room
for you and other friends.
Let me agree to this, agreeably.
It is enough to understand
that, somehow, good was done;
and I, somehow, had helped.

There will be many occasions, Lord,
when you will praise me for my faith.
You do not have to thank me for my hospitality.

Amen.

3

Lady Firstguess

Jesus was at Bethany in the house of Simon the leper; he was at dinner when a woman came in with an alabaster jar of very costly ointment, pure nard. She broke the jar and poured the ointment on his head...

When they saw this, the disciples were indignant: "Why this waste?" they said. "Ointment like this could have been sold for over three hundred denarii and the money given to the poor." And they were angry with her.

But Jesus said, "Leave her alone. Why are you upsetting her? What she has done for me is one of the good works. You have the poor with you always, and you can be kind to them whenever you wish, but you will not always have me. She has done what was in her power to do: she has anointed my body beforehand for its burial.

"I tell you solemnly, wherever throughout all the world the Good News is proclaimed, what she has done will be told also, in remembrance of her."

Mark 14:3-9; Matthew 26:6-13
John 12:1-8

*T*he unnamed person of this story is a lady, like Lady Devirtnoc (Chapter 14). Indeed, there are so many similarities between them, they have frequently been identified. Both women made an uninvited entrance at the house of a man named Simon, while Jesus "was at dinner." Both had an alabaster jar filled with perfume. Both poured this liquid on either the feet or the head of Jesus as an expression of loving care. Both were praised for what they did.

So much for the similarities. There are too many differences between Luke's account and what was written by Mark and Matthew. In Luke, the person was reputedly a sinner, probably a prostitute. There is not even a hint of any sordid past connected with the woman mentioned by Mark and Matthew. Simon the Leper (not Simon the Pharisee, of Luke's story) made no objection of any kind to the person who barged into his house; he made no snide remarks about the character or the surprising gesture of this new member of his dinner party. The querulous comments came from our Lord's Apostles, not from him.

She probably was wealthy — twelve thousand dollars of material poured out "in one shot" is no small thing! She certainly loved Jesus very much. She *most* assuredly did a praiseworthy thing. Jesus spoke of her as he spoke of no one else. His command was addressed to the Apostles... and, from them, to the Church for all time: "I tell you most solemnly, wherever throughout all the world the Good News is proclaimed, what she has done will be told also, in remembrance of her."

The episode took place early in Holy Week. It is linked with our Lord's own burial preparations. Before entombment, every corpse was coated with myrrh or some other kind of spice and then swaddled in a linen cloth. It was the custom of the time. It was considered to be the most important of all "good works." It happened to everybody. Twelve thousand dollars worth, however, did not happen to everybody. Such a lavish amount of "costly ointment, pure nard" was usually reserved for very important people, like the Pharaohs. Jesus understood her action in this context; it was personal worship given to him who was "greater than any Pharaoh."

Only two days later, Jesus celebrated the Passover with his Apostles. There was an unnamed person who figured in that supper, too. (See Chapter 2.) He was as generous as the woman was. Perhaps his was less of a sacrifice of money; but his was a greater sacrifice when one considers the inconvenience to himself and his household staff and the time spent on all the preparatory details. Yet all that he had done was brushed aside, without comment; but all that "she has done must be told, in remembrance of her."

There must be a reason for this strange contrast between our Lord's unremarked acceptance of one person's generosity, and his solemn insistence that another person be publicly praised with unending gratitude.

I must confess, it is easier for me to write about the man who was neglected than to bring up the woman Jesus told me to remember. The host of the Last Supper did admirable things that I can readily approve of; he was generous in ways that can be easily understood. The demands of hospitality have not changed all that much. Twenty centuries after the time of Jesus, we know the price of preparing a special meal for an honored guest. We know the need (it is not a luxury) to create an atmosphere of privacy and leisure when important matters are to be discussed. We know the demands of such solicitation, and we are ready to praise the individual who went to all that trouble. Only the most small-minded of un-Christians would object to the cost of effort, time, and money which made the Last Supper possible. Perhaps this is why Jesus made no solemn injunction that his benefactor of Holy Thursday be praised. The man's generosity would be naturally remembered by all who appreciate warm hospitality.

But the generosity lavished by the woman two days before — this is a different kind of good work altogether. The ointment of nard used up in that brief ministration was worth 300 denarii. That was the salary which an ordinary worker would earn in twelve months. At the modern rate of exchange, the jar of perfume could call for twelve thousand American dollars, give or take a couple of thousand.

Many things could have been done with all that money instead of spilling fluid on someone's head and letting it slip irretrievably to the floor. People were shocked...good people, most of them. St. John's Gospel singles out Judas as the only grumbler: "Why wasn't this ointment sold for 300 denarii and the money given to the poor?"

There were rumblings of indignation on the lips of "some of them," as Mark says, or of everyone, as Matthew says: "When they saw this, the disciples were indignant: 'Why this waste?'"

St. Matthew's version seems to be the fairest one. Perhaps not all of them spoke up, but all shared the blame of the pervading atmosphere of resentment.

The group seems to have been comprised of a wide assortment of second-guessers. To be sure, they all agreed it was a terrible waste of money. To be equally as sure, each one had a different idea of how the money should have been used.

Nobody noticed how the woman was taking all this in . . . nobody, that is, but Jesus. She had just done something beautiful. Rich scent filled the whole room with an aura suggesting peace and wonderful solemnity. Not since the Magi presented him with gold, frankincense, and myrrh had Jesus been so honored. Never had his sacredness and uniqueness been treated with such care. It was a good thing she had done. She was no second-guesser. She knew what was good for Jesus on her first guess.

The Master would rise from the dead, as he had promised. In order to do this, the Master must first die. It would be soon; by a certain grace-given hunch she knew this to be so. No one was worthier than he. Kings and Pharaohs were sumptuously prepared for burial. Here was a Master greater than them all. What is a year's salary when such an occasion calls for the greatest of respects?

She did it. She probably didn't think too much about it. Certainly, she didn't calculate. Prudence was not engaged — worship was. She might have expected the disciples to be pleased by what she did . . . surprised too, perhaps, but mostly pleased. She didn't expect to receive a storm of protest, suggesting that she had terribly misbehaved.

What a letdown. Her generosity was gnawed at by a bunch of second-guessers who thought goodness had better things to do than that! Mark even says that "they were angry with her."

The disciples did not notice her sad face, the desperate panic that showed in her eyes. Apparently, they had neither the time nor the sensitivity to think about how their scolding remarks would affect the woman. They were spending money, imaginary money, on projects of their own devising: "What wonderful things I could do with all those thousands, if only that alabaster jar weren't wasted!"

Jesus was the only one who noticed. "Leave her alone," he commanded. "Why are you upsetting her? She has done me a good work . . . You have the poor with you always and you can be kind to them whenever you wish; but you will not always have me."

The disciples had forgotten that Christianity is not the only important thing; Christ is important, too. Surely, kindness to the poor, projects that work for the betterment of humankind, committees that steer funds to help the disadvantaged — these are all worthy endeavors, endorsed by our Lord himself. But "wasted" time with Jesus in prayer and the "wasted" costly ointment of our worship is worthy too, at times more worthy than all the projects and all the committees in the world.

Lady Firstguess was aware that this particular occasion called for the worship of personal religion, not the philanthropy of good causes. She followed her instinct; she acted on her first impulse. She worshipped our Lord with all she had.

For this she was applauded with a canonization that would stick in the Church's conscience for all time. "What she has done for me," our Lord commanded, "must be told in the same breath that you tell what I have done for you. I want both to be remembered always."

There is a bit of Lady Firstguess in us all. Everyone can identify with her to some extent. We have been impulsively generous at times. We have, also, been upset by other people who second-guessed our motives and scolded us for what we did.

We thought we might have been given a better reception. At great sacrifice of time, effort, and perhaps money too, we went out of our way to help someone. We joined an organization that worked for career developments or for some kind of civic justice or personal growth; we contributed to a noble enterprise. We could't do everything. That would spread us too thin. We did one or two things that seemed to fit our interests, inclinations, time, energy, and wallet. Our motives were good; our cause was a worthy one.

Our endeavors had hardly begun when we discovered how many people could get indignant about it. "You're wasting your time and money!" That's the favorite expression. "Your energy should have been spent doing this or that or some other thing!" That's the second put-down.

Sometimes they even doubt our motives, condemning us for wanting to attract attention, or wanting to manipulate the people we impulsively assisted, or for some other base desire. Such a reaction seems to be implied in the Gospels. The disciples not only resented the waste of money that could have been better used; they also were angry at the woman for making such a display of her munificence.

There have been second-guessers in our lives, too. (There are many more "prudenter-than-thou's" in the world than there are "holier-than-thou's"!) We've been upset by their response no less than the woman who decided to do a good deed for Jesus four days before he died.

Sometimes the let-down we experience comes not so much from a negative "know better" response. Sometimes it comes from no response at all. People from whom we might expect encouragement don't seem to care... don't even seem to notice. This hurts just as much as the expressed indignancies.

It is at such times that we need to cultivate the third part of the woman's personal experience. She not only guessed right about the good thing to be done. She not only felt saddened (indeed, "upset") by the angry reaction that greeted her. She also waited for Jesus to respond. After all, he was the one she was doing it for. His response came quickly, but not so quickly that it prevented her from being hurt by her neighborly know-it-alls. But it did come... of course, in Christ's good time.

She was praised. She was reminded that our Lord would never forget her kindness. This was enough. Let the sideline-quarterbacks criticize her action all they wanted. The only important thing is the approval of the person in whose name the good work was performed. She not only had a singleness of purpose, she also had a more important virtue, one harder to cultivate: a singleness-of-approval-for-the-purpose... which is to say, a detachment from the disapproval of others.

If we can identify with the woman Jesus praised, we can also identify with the men Jesus brought up short. We too have a bit of the "second guesser" in us. Regarding people who have done a good thing, Jesus insists in no uncertain terms that we are to "leave them alone. Do not cause upset. Remember them with gratitude and praise."

It is almost instinctive with us to act like those querulous disciples at times. If someone goes off to the Peace Corps, she should have stayed home. ("There's plenty of injustice right here that she could have been more fittingly involved in!") If the same person stayed home to do that very thing, she should have gone someplace else "where she was more needed."

If a person stays close to the family to support them, he should have lived his own life and let welfare help his parents. If he went away, he was selfish, thinking only of himself.

If a parish decides to build a church, requesting from each parishioner but a small fraction of "300 denarii," the whole area is up in arms about irresponsible expenditure. ("The place of worship could be sold and all that money given to my plans for helping those that interest me!") If the same parish, instead of building the new church, sponsors a particular project, the money was ill-spent: "It should have gone into something else."

Careers with a religious bent suffer most drastically from know-it-all-itis. Humanists have no objection to good works managed as the host of the Last Supper managed them. Hospitality is still an honorable enterprise. Consideration for someone in need, who asks for a favor, as Jesus asked for the use of the upper room, is a praiseworthy thing to do. But fur starts flying when a young woman decides to be a nun. It is even worse when she enters the life of undistracted worship as a contemplative. "Why all this waste?" is the chorus of acrimony. "The thrown-away life is like the thrown-away jar of precious ointment. No good for anything any more. Why weren't those energies harnessed into something more worthwhile?"

Jesus keeps insisting, "Leave her alone. She is doing a good work, caring for my honor with her direct attention. The poor you have always with you. There are many ways and people who will see to their needs. I am important, too. Worship is due me. She should be praised, not criticized."

Jesus keeps insisting on the same thing when decisions to spend time in prayer are domesticated into a little half-hour a day or one evening a week. If an adolescent returns home from a retreat or some other deeply moving experience and spends all his new energy doing more household chores or studying for high honors, this would be commendable. Such practical activity is like the thoughtfulness provided by the host of the Last Supper. But if the youngster also spends time in "unproductive pursuits" like personal meditation or public witness of his faith, the family often gets down on him and flings the word "phony" or "time-waster" in his face.

Let the wife assume a new resolve to go to daily Mass... let the husband decide to go to a Tuesday prayer meeting, or Wednesday choir practice, or take some course to help him know God better, and the offended spouse can sometimes resent it bitterly: "If you have to work overtime on the job, I can understand; if you want to work overtime attending a course on financial improvement, okay; but anything over the bare essentials of devotion is overdoing it!"

For every person who wants to "waste time" with God in simple, unaffected worship, there's a whole cluster of individuals who will try to siphon off this spirituality into some form of pragmatic productivity. If they had their will, Jesus would be left "high and dry," without any ointment of respect or care applied to him personally.

I know a priest who preaches in a stimulating way. He once remarked to me that people often tell him, "Father, you missed your calling; you should have been an actor." The way in which such statements were said made it clear that they were complimentary. The priest would acknowledge them as such, yet I wonder, wistfully, if anybody ever went up to Sir Lawrence Olivier or Red Skelton and said, "Sir, you have such talent and warmth and sensitivity, you missed your calling; you should have been a priest."

Chances are, nobody did. The implication is that a priest, compared to other vocations, is a relative dead-end of talent that could be used more productively in other ways.

"Why all this waste?" is the general response of second-guessers. The particular objection (how energy or money or time or life's career could be better occupied) is different in each case. But it is the general response which Jesus solemnly warns us to avoid. He would have us praise whatever good that is done as good. He would have us especially understand that the good work of prayerful worship is something to remember . . . and remember well.

Prayer of Lady Firstguess Within

Jesus, my Lord,
Please make me more immediate to you.
Don't let too many intermediaries
        work your will around
        to serve their purposes.
The thoughtfulness I do for you is,
            after all, for you
        and not for other people's praise or disapproval.

When I begin to think *I'm* pretty good,
        that's probably my pride.
Then would I do well to listen
        to what second-guessers have to say.
Most likely, they are right
        in their detection of base vanity or arrogance,
        or in their practical suggestions
            about how I could improve behavior.

But when I think of deeds simply as good to do
and do them with instinctive generosity,
        don't let me be upset or feed on doubts
        because some people become indignant
        by what they judge to be a waste;

and angrily declare
I should have been employed in other ways.

And, mostly, when I think of *you* as good,
    spending a generous amount of time
    simply in worship of your sacred graciousness,
        don't let practitioners of a more pragmatic bent
        convince me that I am a wastrel.

Let me be like that woman you commanded to be praised.
Let me hear your kind approval of my personal devotion.
If you are pleased by what I do for you,
    as you,
    I have no need of any other pleasantness.

Amen.

4

Mr. Turnaround

Now on the way to Jerusalem [Jesus] traveled along the border between Samaria and Galilee. As he entered one of the villages, ten lepers came to meet him. They stood some way off and called to him, "Jesus! Master! Take pity on us." When he saw them he said, "Go show yourselves to the priests." Now as they were going away they were cleansed.

Finding himself cured, one of them turned back praising God at the top of his voice and threw himself at the feet of Jesus and thanked him. The man was a Samaritan.

This made Jesus say, "Were not all ten made clean? The other nine, where are they? It seems that no one has come back to give praise to God, except this foreigner." And he said to the man, "Stand up and go on your way. Your faith has saved you."

Luke 17:11-19

As you will see in Chapter 6, the Canaanite woman was a model of good communication. She was an excellent listener, adapting herself to the other person's *words*. The unnamed person in this chapter is her companion. He, too, was a good communicator. With him, it was more in the area of giving — he adapted himself to the other person's *needs*.

I have given him the name "Mr. Turnaround" because he had a turnaround in his life...and after he had it, he gave it.

He was a leper. Twenty centuries ago, lepers were people who suffered in every way possible. Physically, they endured escalating weakness, constant itching, and the pain of unattended sores; they also suffered from lack of food and from the most unhygienic conditions imaginable. Psychologically, they were tormented by their own ugliness, uselessness, and helplessness; they suffered conditions of beggary and the spectre of swift-approaching death.

Socially, they were outcasts; they had to "stand afar off," warning healthy people not to get close to them. They were worse than nobodies — they were "contamination."

Spiritually, they were considered unlovable, even by God. Superstition considered such sickness to be a curse, caused by God as punishment for past misbehavior.

There were ten such lepers, this badly off, who lived near a village bordering Samaria and Galilee. They all must have had some kind of faith. They came, seeking Jesus out. God had worked miracles in the past, and Jesus had already cured a number of people. Besides, what did they have to lose? They came only as close as social custom permitted them, and they shouted, "Jesus! Master! Take pity on us!"

Our Lord's reply was different than usual. For people with withered arms, or blindness, or a sick daughter at home, Jesus spoke the word and, straightaway, the cure took place. This time, because of the stringent law that lepers had to "know their place," Jesus was very law-abiding. He always had his eye out for the enemies who always had their eyes on him. Lepers could not return to normal society unless the priests (who also served as the medical board of that time) gave them a clean bill of health. They could not leave the land of the zombies and enter the world of real people until they passed inspection. So Jesus told them to go through customs. On their way, they were made clean.

This was a turnabout for all ten of them. Their lives were changed completely. What a wonderful feeling it must have been, their bodies fresh and clean and strong again, their blood tingling with new life. They could leap and run and laugh. They probably hugged one another for joy, in the way that football players do when they score a touchdown. Their flesh had been the cause of all their grief; then, thanks to Jesus' cure, it became the source of bright prospects for the future. Life had certainly turned around for them.

But only one of the lepers turned around for the Person who turned his life around.

I'm sure the other lepers thanked Jesus in their own way. I can visualize them, years later, telling the story to a group of fellow-workers or to strangers in some tavern on the main street of Damascus: "Yes, we were lepers once. Then Jesus of Nazareth healed us; our skin became pink and fresh as a healthy baby's. Not sure what happened to the Wonderworker. Understand he got in trouble with the authorities and was put to death. All we can say is that he was kind to us. Whaddya say, fellas, a round of drinks in honor of the good prophet of Nazareth!"

And I am sure they were convinced that "We are thanking Jesus in our own way."

One of the ten, however, thanked Jesus in the way that Jesus could appreciate. He took the trouble to retrace his steps, wade through the crowd, and present himself once more to Jesus. This time, the man came in veneration, not petition. "Finding himself cured, one of them turned back, praising God at the top of his voice . . .and thanked Jesus."

Our Lord must have been pleased by this concrete expression of gratitude. More than pleased, maybe . . . maybe even steadied in his resolve to continue.

St. Luke clearly hints that this event in Christ's life was more than just a minor episode. The Evangelist begins his account of the ten lepers with the often-repeated phrase: "Now, on the way to Jerusalem . . ." It was part of a most significant trip. Jesus knew what would happen at the end of the journey: "As the time drew near for him to be taken up . . . he resolutely set out for Jerusalem" (Luke 9:51). He knew he would be "taken up," raised on the cross and then raised from death and finally raised into heaven. . .ll the events narrated in Chapters 9:51 - 19:27 have an added poignancy to them because they were all part of Luke's "Journey Narrative." The reactions and responses to Jesus during this brief time in his life were understood within a much larger perspective: they were hints, "signs," intimations of how he would be received by all people, for all time, even after he had healed the spiritual leprosy of the whole world by his redemptive passion.

It is not hard, therefore, to imagine the sadness in our Lord's eyes when he saw only one of the ten return. The modulation of his voice may have been muted, as though a cosmic ingratitude took some of the wind out of his lungs. The words suggest such an interpretation. Jesus asked the good leper: "Were not all ten made clean? Where are the other nine? Has no one come back to give praise to God, except this (one)?"

Our Lord, of course, did not work the cure only for the sake of having the lepers thank him, any more than he would cure our hopelessness just so we would be appreciative. All ten were cured — all people are redeemed — whether all thank him or not.

But it had to hurt when he realized he was forgotten so quickly by nine out of ten people — 9/10ths of the world, if this was a hint of things to come. And it had to be a good experience (perhaps a saving one for the human nature of Christ) that at least one returned to give him thanks.

There was contact made with someone who had a heart big enough to make contact in return. There was the shout of a man's voice, the love of joy in his eyes, the words and gestures expressed in a way that Jesus could perceive and take comfort in. The whole bearing of the man proclaimed: "I was a hopeless leper, and you, Lord, made me different and gave me new life. I have you to thank for it...and I will praise you forever, with all my heart!"

One out of ten! Jesus had wished for more, but even one was worth it. He continued on his journey to Jerusalem. He continues, still, to give all people healing and new life even when we seem to take it for granted.

But there is a special place in his heart for those who respond as the good leper did. "Your faith has saved you," Jesus said to Mr. Turnaround. "You are not only cured, you're saved. By taking the trouble to thank me, contact is made both ways. You, now, cannot forget me any more than I can forget you. This is what it means to be saved. Stand up and go in peace."

The thanks-giving spirit of the good leper is a spirit that we all have, at least on certain occasions. When birthdays come, or anniversaries, or Christmas especially, most people work out of the grateful side of their personality.

We don't think about "What's in it for us?" when we plan our Christmas shopping list. We think of those we love...we put ourselves in their shoes...we try to sense their needs, not ours. This is an occasion to thank friends and relatives for their love. Our concern is "What will please them?" We don't mind the shopping or the drain on our wallet. We don't mind any more than the good leper minded his long trip back to Jesus and the bother of wading through the crowd to thank him personally. We care; and we want to give some kind of visible sign of our gratitude in a way that the other person will appreciate.

But special occasions are one thing; ordinary routine is something else. On ordinary occasions, the nine-leper style of heedlessness is often the pattern. When people show us kindness we may very well be thankful "in our own fashion." But we often neglect to let them know our gratitude in any palpable way that they can relish. Such negligence amounts to taking them for granted. From their point of view, it seems as though we just expected to be treated considerately as we went off on our merry own way . . . taking, but not returning to give thanks.

Certainly, the friend didn't do us that favor for the sole purpose of getting gratitude in return any more than Jesus cured all ten lepers for that purpose. Just the same, it hurts to be slighted, or to feel "used." More sadness has come from heedlessness than perhaps from any other source.

For this reason, as well as for the simple rightness of it, it would be well to cultivate the spirit of Mr. Turnaround in our ordinary relationships. It may be that we are "one out of ten" people who give thanks to somebody. It may be that our expressions of practical gratitude will be enough to keep them going. At least somebody cares that they have cared.

What is true for ordinary people, on ordinary occasions, is also true for Jesus. Our Lord still has reason to lament the fact that so few people take the trouble to return to him with expressions of gratitude that he can understand. Many people are convinced that they thank him "in their own way" — when the mood suits them, when a wonderful experience attracts them to quiet veneration, or when special urgency or festival scoots them off to church. But if that is all it is, it's no better than the gratitude expressed by the nine lepers of the Gospel. Such sporadic demonstrations do not show that these people think much about God as such. They only think of self — the convenience, the promptings, the needs of self.

The giving of thanks is a delicate skill. It is another aspect of communication. Just as the listening skill demands that we put ourselves into the head of the other person and hear what is said as the other person meant it, so the "thanksgiving skill" shows appreciation in ways that will stimulate joy and gladness in the giver.

Jesus has left us with no doubt about the fact that he is pleased when we return to him with praise. In other places of the Gospel, he has told us how to do it. We are to remember him. We are to think of him. (In Old English language, the words think and thank were the same; today as well, thoughtfulness is the best expression of thankfulness.)

It is not easy to be thoughtfully thankful. It is not easy to remember Jesus, his way. Sometimes it is a bother to set regular time aside for prayer. Sometimes it is too much of a drain on our time to study the Scriptures; we'd rather do something else. Often, it is tempting not to go to church because we are "not getting anything out of it!"

Even so. Even when we don't get anything out of it, these are still the ways that make Jesus glad-of-heart for having journeyed to Jerusalem to be raised up for our sakes. He has already cured us. But he cannot keep in contact with us unless we keep in contact with him. The good leper made contact by coming back to Jesus and giving thanks. We make contact the very same way . . . only we must do it much more thoughtfully, having more grounds for gratitude than even he had.

Prayer of Mr. Turnaround Within

Jesus, my Lord,
Make me a turner-back to you.
Mind me of my heedlessness
    — the spirit of those other lepers
    who just kept going on their way
    without a thought of you.

Let me remember your ways with me.
All the ways you have been kind
    and cleansing-good;
    especially that way which was your journey to Jerusalem.

Let me return, re-think, and think again
    about your curing care
    which healed me of those sores
    that had made me an outcast from myself
    as well as from you.

You put new life in me.
You made me feel as fresh as baby's skin,
    full of life's possibilities,
    hopeful,
    able to be loved, and loving.
Let me remember it was you who did it.

By prayer,
    by study of your words,
    and by the way I worship you out loud, at public liturgy,
    let me turn 'round
        to thank you for the reasons of my gratitude.
And, as I keep developing this skill,
    let me be more skilled in all my thoughtfulness:
Not just remembering my friends on great occasions,
    but also for those kindnesses that I take so for granted;
    let me acknowledge favors done
    in such ways that they can understand
    how much it meant to me.

Thus I will dedicate myself to thankfulness.
With such good thoughts as these
    I will save my faith in you;
    and it is faith that will save me.

Amen.

5

Mr. Gofrom

They reached the country of the Gerasenes on the other side of the lake and no sooner had Jesus left the boat than a man with an unclean spirit came out from the tombs towards him. The man lived in the tombs and no one could secure him any more, even with a chain; because he had often been secured with fetters and chains but had snapped the chains and broken the fetters and no one had the strength to control him. All night and all day, among the tombs and in the mountains, he would howl and gash himself with stones. Catching sight of Jesus from a distance, he ran up and fell at his feet and shouted at the top of his voice, "What do you want with me, Jesus, son of the Most High God? Swear by God you will not torture me!" "What is your name?" Jesus asked. "My name is legion," he answered, "for there are many of us."

Now there was there on the mountainside a great herd of pigs feeding, and the unclean spirit begged him, "Send us to the pigs, let us go into them." So he gave them leave. With that, the unclean spirits came out and went into the pigs, and the herd of about two thousand pigs charged down the cliff into the lake, and there they were drowned...

People came to see what had happened...and they saw the demoniac sitting at the feet of Jesus, clothed and in his full senses...

As Jesus was getting into the boat, the man who had been possessed begged to be allowed to stay with him. Jesus would not let him but said to him, "Go home to your people and tell them all that the Lord in his mercy has done for you." So the man went off...

Mark 5:1-20; Luke 8:26-39
Matthew 8:28-34

The three Gospels call him simply "a man with an unclean spirit." Tradition has called him the "Gerasene Demoniac" because he was possessed by devils and he happened to live in a place called "the country of the Gerasenes on the other side of Lake Galilee."

I would like to give him the name "Mr. Gofrom." It indicates the good side of his personality he finally wound up with. If the man had his preference, he would have settled for the name "Mr. Stayput." This indicates the bad side of his character. He first demanded to remain depressed; he then pleaded to remain consoled. He was not allowed either stability.

Without doubt, he wanted to stay put, and he wanted this intensely. With just a small assortment of picture-words — tombs, mountains, snapped chains, howling and gashing with stones, no one with the strength to control him — the Gospels begin the story by describing a man who had a terrible opinion about everybody. He was a loner, filled with a frenzy of self-hatred. He was uncontrollable; no chains (probably no words of kindness, either) could influence him in any way at all. Something inside of him put his life on a course of self-debasement and wild outpourings of rage. Apparently, the man himself determined to hold this course forever.

Yet something else in him was working, too. When Jesus arrived, the man's response seems to be completely negative: "What do you want with me, Jesus, Son of the Most High God? I beg you, do not torture me!"

On the surface, this is a rousing unwelcome. Like all the other possessed people in the Gospel, this man wanted Jesus to "get out" . . . to "leave me alone!" Yet the last verb used has to cause some kind of wonder. Why did he say, "Don't torture me!" What could the torture be? The man had been torturing himself for many years. Then Jesus came, offering to untorture him . . . and this was claimed to be a torture.

There seems to have been two spirits battling inside him for control. One spirit saw intuitively that Jesus could give him peace. Once at peace, he could admit again that he was worthwhile. From this consideration might flow the possibility that he could accept other people's kindness and be kind to them. One side of him wanted to be healed.

The other side — the one represented by the legion of devils inside him — did not want anything to happen. This side wanted to stand pat in bitter rage and uncontrollable unhappiness. It is difficult to change any strongly developed attitude or pattern of behavior. It is most difficult when the attitude is self-hatred and the behavior patterns are those of anger and despair.

Change would have to come about if Jesus were to be permitted to work his ways with the man. There was an appeal in the word "torture." It was as if the man said, "I want to change. I want to be at peace and live in such a way that kindness, joy, and mutual respect will sit comfortably with me. But I'm terribly afraid, too. I'm so used to feeling sorry for myself and hating everything around me, I'm afraid I'll be left with nothing if I let go of the power which comes from my resentment!"

It seems that part of him wanted to be changed. But most of him wanted things just as they were; even though he was miserable, he was used to it.

Jesus would not let him stay that way. Sometimes, kindness has the jolting effect of a command. It was so in this case. The demons of debasement were evicted. St. Mark mentions that "about 2,000 pigs" were needed to carry off the exchange. Without going into all the interpretations of this strange fact, two things are clear: 1) the force that was energizing his anger was a very powerful one; 2) he must have been a very powerful man to contain this energy and still be alive at all.

Once the devils left, peace came. A sense of quiet settled in, the stillness that comes after a storm. "They saw the demoniac sitting there, clothed, and in his full senses." St. Luke adds an important clue. He notes that the man was "sitting at the feet of Jesus." Discipleship is clearly hinted at.

It is not surprising that he should switch from one allegiance to another. He was still a man of strength, vigorously forceful in his certainties. Only now, his forcefulness had a different focus. Before, he had intensely acted out what he had received from the devils of despair. Now, he wanted to stay put once more, intensely acting out what he had received from Jesus. According to St. Mark, the man "begged to be allowed to stay with him."

"Please," he pleaded, "please let me stay with you." But the Lord said no. He refused him. Simple as that! "Jesus would not let him (stay) but said to him, 'Go home to your people and tell them all what the Lord in his mercy has done for you'."

What a letdown. To go home. To assume a life not of his own choosing. Not to follow his natural bent. Not to stay in the environment where he could be just as certain of his worth as he used to be certain of his worthlessness. Go back to the ho-hum world, to an unimaginative career, to the lukewarm people who were only half-heartedly interested in any cause, any cause at all.

He had to return to the towns he lived in before he became possessed. He laid the groundwork for the future spreading of the Gospel. Perhaps, as he walked away from the shore, his words were, "I must tell the story — over and over and over — about how God has shown mercy to me. I must answer those questions (they will sound like such repetitions soon): 'Were you really that crazy?' 'Did you really live in caves?' 'Were there really all those swine that were drowned in the water?' And that most difficult question of all: 'If you love Jesus so much, why didn't you stay with him?' And I'll have to answer, 'because he didn't want me to. He wanted me to do this instead'."

It had to be a hard assignment for such a warm enthusiast. He seems to have done a very good job. By the time the Book of Revelations was written, 50 years or so afterward, the same ten towns had thriving Christian communities. He did what he had to. He took Christ's no for the answer. He may have preferred to be another person, to live another way, to feel that his rich potential was being fulfilled. But Jesus placed him in other circumstances, and — may Mr. Gofrom be praised forever — he did a good job at what he was given to do.

Everyone has a different range of depression/elation. Many people may not have the same emotional intensity of the possessed man in the Gospel. Even so, we have all experienced "downs" in our life, and the "ups" that followed them; to some degree, we've wanted to stay put with one, then with the other.

We may not have sunk as deeply into feelings of rage or self-disgust. But we have known the feelings, somehow. We may never have lived in caves or been so angry that nobody could control us, but we've wanted to, at times. Unyielding loneliness is not a stranger to anyone; even small children feel the pain of it. We have all had our moments of frenzied desperation, bitterness that possessed every space in our hearts, broodings that grew so out-of-control that nobody could restrain us, either by chains or kindness.

Then, somehow, into our lives came change, and we, somehow, let it happen. Feelings and attitudes had a turnabout: instead of frenzy, we enjoyed a sense of peace; instead of anger caught in a web of aimlessness, we felt a desire to use our newly-found potential for the betterment of others or for dedication to an ideal.

Jesus can use many different movements or situations to effect such a transition in us. Everyone is different; we have different ways of reaching new insights and fresh enthusiasms. Some have made a retreat, or marriage encounter, or cursillo, or a secular workshop, or have been prayed over by charismatics. Some have been touched by a kind confessor, an understanding parent, a gifted teacher. Some have fallen in love, or found a cause that turned their dreadfully boring existence into a life filled with exciting possibilities.

However the change in us occurred, it was a beautiful experience. It gave us what the masters of spiritual life call "sensible consolation." When such a wonderful thing happens, the tendency is to want to "stay put," as Peter, James, and John wanted to remain on Mt. Tabor, and as the Gerasene demoniac wanted to remain sitting at the feet of Jesus.

It is a natural tendency, this desire to never leave the circumstances that put peace in our hearts. Sometimes, of course, it is right to continue with our newly-discovered source of nourishment. Second careers are sometimes a good idea. Sudden interest in new goals, and new forms of Christian dedication, can be graces we must follow up on with all the verve we can muster, enjoying all the fresh vigor it can bring.

But sometimes it is not right to remain where we first found our reborn spirit. Consolations may leave us and circumstances move us past the sensible delights we once enjoyed, sending us into a career with less relish to it, with people we don't find as compatible as before. It may simply be a case, spiritually or literally, of finding that "the honeymoon is over" and we must make the best of our ho-hum world and yet never lose our gratitude for past graces.

It is impossible to fully understand God's ways with us. We can be no more than cautiously provisional; sometimes the Lord wants this, sometimes that; sometimes these words of our Lord apply, sometimes those.

The character study of Mr. Gofrom points out one of these "sometimes truths." Sometimes Jesus refuses to comply with our wishes that we do certain things, in a certain way, with a certain preferred group of people, who will reproduce the good feelings we had when we first felt peace.

Sometimes God says no to our wishes to stay put at the place where there is warmth and certainty. When he says no, it may be that he means it. But with the no, there is always a yes that he wants us to say to something else.

Prayer of Mr. Gofrom Within

Jesus, my Lord,
    you know me inside out
    and upside-down
    and downside-up
    ...especially downside-up.
You know how often I let my enthusiasms
    get the best, and the worst, of me.

You know how I get down at times,
    out-of-control with misery and outrage
    (almost as bad as the man you cured so long ago).
And then I feel a peace come over me,
    thanks to a special, sacred time of grace...
And I am up again,
    sitting comfortably,
    controlled,
    and with all my senses.
I've gone from down to up,
    and in my fresh enthusiasm
I want to make sure nothing ever stops.
I want to further all these gifts,
    developing more fervently this high exhilaration,
    becoming a relisher of moments,
    never quitting what feels so good to keep.

And sometimes you say no.
My way of being your disciple must be some other way
    — a way I won't have nearly so much ready warmth about.
These are the times I need to understand you:
    when your no really means no,
    no matter how unselfish and how noble are my hopes.
I need the spirit of the man you cured from aimlessness,
    and then to have an aim (to be with you)
    and then let that be cancelled out
    for a humbler, less preferred one.

Let me agree to this
    when the times come for it to happen.
Let me not go from out-of-control in madness
    to too-much-control in specified desires.

Let me stay loose and unpossessed
    by any of my enthusiasms:
So that I may be freed, even from my best intentions,
So that I may be, then, possessed by you,
    and you alone,
    and what it is that you would have me do.

Amen.

6
Mrs. Comeback

Jesus withdrew to the region of Tyre and Sidon. Then out came a Canaanite woman from that district and started shouting, "Sir, Son of David, take pity on me. My daughter is tormented by the devil." But he answered her not a word. And his disciples went and pleaded with him. "Give her what she wants," they said, "because she is shouting after us." He said in reply, "I was sent only to the lost sheep of the House of Israel."

But the woman had come up and was kneeling at his feet. "Lord," she said, "help me." He replied, "It is not fair to take the children's food and throw it to the house-dogs." She retorted, "Ah yes, sir; but even house-dogs can eat the scraps that fall from their master's table." Then Jesus answered her, "Woman, you have great faith. Let your wish be granted . . . you may go home happy . . ."

And from that moment her daughter was well again.

Matthew 15:21-28
Mark 7:24-30

*T*his chapter is a companion-piece to the one before it. The woman I call "Mrs. Comeback" is as strong a character as Mr. Gofrom.

There is this big difference: the man wanted to follow Jesus and was refused; he took this no for the answer, adjusting his life accordingly. The woman under study here was also refused. Jesus said no just as surely; and in this case the no was stated without any cushion of alternatives ("I don't want you to do this; I want you to do that") — it was a straight, flat no, expressed in such a way that it could easily be interpreted as an insult.

The woman did not take this no for an answer. She came back with her prayer. She rearranged the wording of the request. Flexibility and wit were as much her attributes as was resiliency. Jesus changed his mind; he turned his no into a yes, although it seemed that he had not planned to do so.

Here is another "sometimes truth" of Christianity: sometimes we are to keep plugging away with our petitions until God gives in to our appeals.

The situation could have turned out otherwise if Mrs. Comeback did not have that good come-back-ability of hers. She was extremely upset about her daughter's debility. "Tormented by the devil" is the way the mother put it. It could have been palsy, epilepsy, a form of depression that accompanies puberty...no one knows. Whatever it was, mother was worried sick about it. Then up to the strange land of the pagans came a stranger who was already famous for miracles among his fellow-Jews. His presence gave her hope for healing that she (Jew or no Jew) was not going to let pass by.

She must have made a pest of herself by her persistent cries. The disciples say as much. They appealed to our Lord to work the cure, not because they cared about her, but because they wanted to be rid of the sound of her outcries. Jesus did not even acknowledge her. He spoke to his disciples about his mission that was reserved only to Israel. Our Lord's top priority was to establish his credentials as the promised Messiah of the Jews. Only after Easter would he permit his significance to "fan out"...to be understood as Savior of all humankind.

The woman was snubbed, but this did not stop her. She forced recognition and personally made her plea. It was brief and to the point: "Lord, help me." Jesus answered her, "No." He did this by means of a *mashal* (or "saying") which served as the reason for his refusal: "As parents give good food only to the children, not to the lesser animals, so my signs of healing are given only to those people who can understand the significance of my cures, not to pagans who can only think of me as some kind of flashy wonderworker."

There are two ways of interpreting Christ's refusal. One way would be: "Jesus just called me and my people dogs. Oh, he couched it a little gently, calling us house pets; but it was still an ethnic slur! He plays up to his favorites, just like other ministers of religion! He doesn't care about us poor people, us nobodies. Just like all the rest of them! He refused me and insulted me in the bargain. Well, I quit! I'm not praying to his God any more either! I'm going to dig a hole into my hurt feelings and stay there nursing the wounds of my refusal and never come out!"

That is one way of interpreting Jesus' words. The other way is to do just what Mrs. Comeback did. She paid close attention to what Jesus was saying. She really listened. She transferred the focus of attention from herself and her concerns to our Lord and his concerns. She was truly an expert in communication. She had highly developed listening skills and empathy. She could walk in the other person's sandals; she could feel things from the other person's point of view.

So far in the story, she had only spoken (to the point of pestering) about her own distress. For the longest time, she and her child were all that filled her mind. But Jesus changed the subject. He spoke of other children, of the House of Israel. This was his overriding preoccupation. She adapted to him, with humility, delicacy, and wit: "Yes, Lord, I understand your interests. But continue your own line of thinking and you will see where I fit in — for children of every family give scraps of food to their favorite household pets."

Our Lord's response is, at first, surprising: "Woman, you have great faith." One could understand him saying that she had great persistence, genuine wit, commendable flexibility, or even debating skills. But why did he mention faith?

It seems that from our Lord's point of view faith was the most important quality. The others were included in it. For a year or so, ever since he began his ministry, Jesus had been faced with the proud spirit of the Pharisees, the spirit of self-preoccupation. They concentrated on themselves, on what they had done for God, on how well they followed the laws and all the minutiae of traditions. They had done all this; therefore God had to reward them. They did not consider themselves servants of God, or children. They acted as though they were "religious loan sharks," doing God favors and expecting to be paid on time, according to their demands. They were not like little children who sometimes have the "gimmies;" they were like arrogant grownups who had the "gottas" (God has "gotta" do

this for me, "gotta" do that for me). Our Lord simply could not relate
to people with the "gottas."

This is why Jesus insisted over and over that "Unless we become
like little children, we shall not enter his Kingdom" (Matthew 18:5,
Mark 9:37; Luke 9:48). Children know that they are on the receiving
end of favors. They are not entitled to rewards. They don't earn
things — they are given things, graced with things.

We must understand that our relationship to God is this kind of
given relationship. There is no more parity of roles between God and
ourselves than there is between parents and their small children.
Unless we understand this, our religion is a farce. The Pharisees had
made a farce, not of God, but of their puffed-up selves. The pagan
woman was by comparison a breath of fresh air. She had this basic
faith, this attitude of being on the receiving end. God, in that case,
can begin his work of giving.

Mrs. Comeback continued with Christ's line of thinking and went
on from there. Following the lead of Jesus' words, she said (in so
many words), "Puppy dogs under the table are even more on the
receiving end than children who give them scraps of food from the
table. I do not say you've got to answer my prayers, Lord. I only said
I need it; I ask you to help me."

St. Mark remembers that our Lord's last word was happy:
"Woman, you may go home happy." I think Jesus ended the scene
this way because the happy feeling was as much his as it was hers,
because he met a person who understood his main concerns, who
was humble, who was not "touchy"... and who knew how not to
take no for an answer.

Everyone is included. If we don't have the "spirit of Mrs. Comeback" in us, we had better develop it. Prayer is impossible without it.

Even ordinary communication — relating with human friends — is
impossible without the qualities demonstrated by this unnamed
woman of the Gospels.

So very often we have developed the other extreme. Instead of
listening to the other person, we tend to keep the focus on ourselves.
Instead of being able to enter another person's feelings ("walking in
their shoes," "understanding where they are coming from," accepting the possibility that their concerns may be different from ours) we
often stay with our own preoccupation and either scold the other for
not understanding us, or walk away in a huff because they seem to

refuse to do so. Then it is not a matter of our bouncing back; it is the other person who must engineer the comeback, after we've gotten over our hurt feelings.

Regarding communication with God in prayer, it is even more important that we subdue our self-preoccupation and develop those resilient qualities that only faith can bring. Let us express our needs, honestly and forcefully, as the woman did. Let us develop a listening capacity, the ability to be open to the possibility that Jesus' way of viewing the matter may be different from ours. Let us persevere, without any trace of touchiness over what may seem to be Christ's snub to our appeals. And above all — and included in them all — let our prayer be grounded in a spirit of faith that puts our hands palms up, a spirit of faith that knows ourselves as little children, on the receiving end, hoping for favors that will come to us...as long as we don't think we "have them coming to us."

Prayer of Mrs. Comeback Within

Jesus, my Lord,
    give me the bounce of Mrs. Comeback.
Let me, in my prayers to you,
    never say die
    ...and never say "got to" either.

Let me be a little child with God, your Father:
    expecting the best, always
    (though I don't always know exactly what this is).

Let me be even a puppy dog in faith:
    who, when brushed aside,
    keeps wagging his tail
    with hope for favorable response.

Replace my touchy heart with ready ears
    attentive to your ultimate concerns,
    which sometimes can be so opposed
    to the immediacy of my requests.
Let me be modified by what I hear from you
    and, rather than leaving in a huff,
    or quitting prayer,

swing my course over to your direction
and change the way I ask for favors
until my wants line up with what you will
...so that you can be happy,
finally,
to grant my prayers,
now asked in the right way.

And let me,
    from this learning of my listening skills with you
Develop these same skills with others,
    especially those I'm close to.
Let me be not so occupied about myself
    that I don't hear them speaking of their needs
    or cannot celebrate with them their joys.

Let me not be so sensitive
    that I hear their no's and never's
    and give up on them,
        nursing their refusals as though they were my wounds.
Let me return, again and again, as Mrs. Comeback did.

And mostly, let me return, again and again, to you,
    showing in my heart a welcome (like a wagging tail);
    having my palms upturned, in a receiving gesture;
    asking you never to quit on me
    because I do not quit on you —
    because, by faith, I know that you want to, and will,
        make me happy.

Amen.

7

Balance Humor

As Jesus went along, he saw a man who had been blind from birth. His disciples asked him, "Rabbi, who sinned, this man or his parents, for him to have been born blind?" "Neither he nor his parents sinned," Jesus answered. "He was born blind so that the works of God might be displayed..."

Having said this, he spat on the ground, made a paste with the spittle, put this over the eyes of the blind man, and said to him, "Go and wash in the Pool of Siloam... So the man went off and washed himself, and came away with his sight restored.

His neighbors and people who earlier had seen him begging said, "Isn't this the man who used to sit and beg?" ... The man himself said, "I am the man." So they said to him, "Then how do your eyes come to be open?" "The man called Jesus," he answered, "made a paste, daubed my eyes with it and said to me, 'Go and wash at Siloam;' so I went, and when I washed I could see..."

They brought the man who had been blind to the Pharisees. It had been a sabbath day when Jesus made the paste and opened the man's eyes, so when the Pharisees asked him how he had come to see, he said, "He put a paste on my eyes, and I washed, and I can see..." So they spoke to the blind man again, "What have you to say about him yourself, now that he has opened your eyes?" The man replied, "He is a prophet."

However, the Jews would not believe that the man had been blind and had gained his sight, without first sending for his parents and asking them, "Is this man really your son who you say was born blind? If so, how is it that he is now able to see?" His parents answered, "We know he is our son and we know he was born blind, but we don't know how it is that he can see now, or who opened his eyes. He is old enough; let him speak for himself."

His parents spoke like this out of fear of the Jews, who had already agreed to expel from the synagogue anyone who should acknowledge Jesus as the Christ. This was why his parents said, "He is old enough; ask him."

So the Jews again sent for the man and said to him: "Give glory to God! For our part, we know that this man is a sinner." The man answered, "I don't know if he is a sinner! I only know that I was blind and now I can see." They said to him, "What did he do to you? How did he open your eyes?" He replied, "I have told you once and you wouldn't listen. Why do you want to hear it all again? Do you want to become his disciples too?" At this they hurled abuse at him: "You can be his disciple," they said, "we are disciples of Moses; we know that God spoke to Moses, but as for this man, we don't know where he comes from." The man replied, "Now here is an astonishing thing! He has opened my eyes, and you don't know where he comes from! We know that God doesn't listen to sinners, but God does listen to men who are devout and do his will. Ever since the world began it is unheard of for anyone to open the eyes of a man who was born blind; if this man were not from God, he couldn't do a thing."

"You are trying to teach us," they replied, "and you a sinner through and through, since you were born!" And they drove him away.

Jesus heard they had driven him away, and when he found him he said to him, "Do you believe in the Son of Man?" "Sir," the man replied, "tell me who he is so that I may believe in him." Jesus said, "You are looking at him; he is speaking to you." The man said, "Lord, I believe," and worshipped him.

John 9:1-38

*I*f I had the freedom to do so, I would name the central figure of this story "The Good Humor Man." Humor was his most important characteristic. He was a good man, too, very good, considering the odds against him and the antagonism fomented by his own family as well as his foes.

But Good Humor Man is a trade name already taken by certain ice cream vendors. Instead, I've given him the first name Balance. He was balanced in his judgments about people and in his assessment about one very eventful afternoon of his life.

Everybody was trying to knock him off his balance, so that he would succumb to their biases of perception. He would not fall. Humor kept him buoyed up.

It must have been disheartening. First everybody, then his own parents, and finally all the notable, religious leaders of Jerusalem — each group, in its own way — tried to unbalance him and force him to admit he was not worthwhile.

The "everybody" even included Christ's own followers: "The disciples asked Jesus, 'Rabbi, who has sinned, this man or his parents, for him to have been born blind?'" Bad health, like bad luck, was supposed to have been a deserving thing; it was considered punishment from a vindictive God. Blindness was thought to be a curse. People of that time, even good people, were superstitious. They interpreted maladies very narrowly. Like Job's comforters, they were at pains to justify God's ways to the human race...but they did so from a materialistic point of view that excluded everything but here-and-now pain or pleasure. "God is good!" they thumped with all their energy. "Therefore, if a person experiences something bad, like blindness, the person must be bad!"

All horizons of hope are blocked off by such narrowness of mind. God's creative possibilities are ignored. God's gradual revelation of life after death, and of his use of sickness as a test for loyalty, or (in the case of a cure) the sign of his overwhelming care — these options were not open to God, according to this thinking. God was just pushed out of the picture, made to stay up in his own corner of heaven. God was simply supposed to "be good"...and let humans work out their dread of sickness by superstitiously labeling lepers, the blind, and the deaf as pariahs who justly merited their misfortune.

Jesus spread out the horizons so that we can let the true God speak for himself about death and other less fatal ailments. God's statement about death was to come later, with the passion, death, and resurrection of his Son. One of the statements about lesser ailments was made in this episode. Jesus said to his disciples: "Neither he nor his parents sinned. He was born blind so that the works of God might be displayed in him." The instant cure of the man's prolonged blindness would be a sacrament of God's care for all our woes, and a sign that only God can give us vision into anything.

No dialogue followed. Jesus made a statement that was not open to argument or debate. The words he said were intended to put to rest forever our superstitious thinking that "Bad luck has come to me because God hates me for something that I or others have done wrong."

Jesus made a paste out of his own spittle and the dirt by the roadside. He put the paste on the man's eyes. Still blind, the beggar groped to the pool of Siloam and followed directions. He went. He washed. He saw. Simple as that.

But the repercussions were not that simple. The man had to keep all of his balance, and all of his wits, to stay true to his experience. He told the inquisitive neighbors the story that he would have to tell over and over: "The man called Jesus did something to my eyes and then told me to do something. I did. I went. I washed. I saw."

The Pharisees found out about it and they did not like it, not at all. Jesus' growing popularity and independence of thought were most distasteful to them. And now he does manual work on the sabbath! He is a paste-maker on the day of rest! When people are desperate in their dislike, they will snatch at anything. They decided that this 30-second labor of love on the sabbath would serve as proof of Christ's disloyalty to the Law of Moses.

A group of them marched forward to put the "fear of the Pharisees" into the healed man. It must have been intimidating. He was outnumbered. There was no doubt about the answer he was supposed to give, if he knew what was good for him. He gave a different answer. It was direct, irrefutable, and most unpopular: "The man who cured me is a prophet of God."

The Pharisees tried another attack. Their arsenal was formidable and they were not to be denied. Jesus' character had to be smeared before it was too late. They tried to browbeat the parents of the man born blind. This time they were somewhat successful.

Only somewhat so. They didn't meet anyone willing to be a character assassin; they didn't meet any opposition either. They met two frightened people who had the personality of blah, the enthusiasm of a dull thud, and a kind of culpable negligence that could almost be called child abuse.

Their son was no longer a child; but he was once. Besides, as far as his vision was concerned, he was like a new-born baby. They did not actually strike their son with blows; but *not caring* is sometimes the form of abuse that takes longest to heal.

Assuredly, for years and years, they had prayed to God for a miracle. Perhaps by now they had given up. They had settled into a groove. "Not to be inconvenienced" was first among all their priorities. They did not want to be put off from their normal routine. They would take no risks, even if it meant snubbing their own son.

St. John indicates their fear by the laconic statement: "His parents spoke like this out of fear of the (leaders of the) Jews, who already agreed to expel from the synagogue anyone who should acknowledge Jesus as the Christ. This was why his parents said, 'He is old enough; ask him.'"

Living in today's world which adheres to a strict division between Church and State, it is difficult to understand the force of such a threat. People today may never enter church or synagogue; they are not excluded from society because of it. They may still join the bowling league or the country club. They may buy and sell real estate. They can go shopping without fear of harassment.

Such was not the case in Israel twenty centuries ago. "Out of the synagogue" meant out of everything. For the two people in question, it meant not only that they would be banished from public worship; it also meant no more Tuesday night bingo games (or the equivalent at that time), no easy-going chatter enjoyed while shopping at the local stores, no permission to build that lovely home in suburban Jerusalem. Son or no son, they weren't going to let any passing enthusiasm deprive them of those comforts.

The man born blind had to have great balance to withstand this crushing blow. His own parents wouldn't get involved! They refused to join him in his joy. It should have been their happiness as well.

Jesus depends upon our natural, human tendency to celebrate good fortune when he speaks of a shepherd rejoicing with friends after finding a lost sheep, of a woman throwing a big party because she found a lost coin, of an expansive father killing the fatted calf when his prodigal son returned home. (All from Luke's Gospel, Chapter 15.)

Here is a case of their own son who now has new eyes to see with and new life to hope for. Instead of jumping for joy and bringing out the best wine to celebrate what truly amounts to commencement exercises, they dismiss their offspring with one cold reference that he is of age and able to manage by himself.

Their action was irresponsible, cowardly, and devastating to their son. It must have hurt him, but it didn't break his spirit. He somehow was able to keep his balance . . . even his humor.

The humor shows up when the Pharisees return, in the last act, to drill him into docility. One can almost hear the sadistic tones of a torturer spitting out those derisive words: "Give glory to God!" (as if to say 'Shut up; I'm going to tell you just once and you better go along with it!') "We ourselves know that this man Jesus is a sinner!"

One can almost see ten pairs of eyes glaring at him, like the spotlights of a "third degree"...all driving him to speak their lie. He would not budge. He refused to deny his own experience: "This one thing I know: I once was blind and now I see...and the man called Jesus did it!"

They pressed him further. Surely he would realize how foolish it would be to lose the friendship of people powerful enough to cut him off from social graces and financial improvement. "What did he do to you?" they insisted. "How did he open your eyes?"

At that point, the man began to see the humor (or, rather, the farce) of the whole interrogation. "What's the sense of repeating it?" the man said. Then, just to enjoy seeing them squirm in their spitefulness, he began his own line of questioning. "Why do you want to hear it again? Do you want to become his disciples, too?"

All their venom exploded on that remark: "We know that God chose Moses; we know such is not the case with Jesus!" The man retained his balance and his position. He even seemed to enjoy the sudden reversal of roles. Common sense began to lecture the wisdom of the wise: "We know God does not listen to sinners, but God does listen to men who are devout and do his will. Ever since the world began it is unheard of for anyone to open the eyes of a man who was born blind; if this man were not from God, he couldn't do a thing."

The Pharisees' last retort was a parting shot of total exasperation. They were like children who have lost an argument and resort to slinging insults at their antagonist: "You were altogether born in sin and do you presume to teach us?"

Then they turned him out. He was on their hate-list from then on. A lesser person would have been crushed: his family had nothing to do with him because of social pressure, and all opportunities for acceptance into the normal world of Jerusalem were forfeited by his presuming to teach his betters.

Yet, somehow, he refused to let such sadness get him down. He knew what had happened to him, and he knew Jesus was to thank for it. These two undeniable facts were his balancing pole. Let family punish him with silence, let the notables punish him with social ostracism. He had no power over what they did...or didn't do. The strong pressure from powerful people did not dismay him. He was in charge of his own certitude. From this advantage, he could see the incongruous illogic of his adversaries. It is no wonder that the last we see of this unnamed man of the Gospels is his gesture of accepting Jesus completely: "and falling down, he worshipped him."

It is easy to become unbalanced. We all have "pools" of hurts that dwell deep in our hearts. They are the remember-able residue of those times when we were put down, made to feel useless or sinful, cut off from social acceptance.

The "pools of sadness" are the things that make each new experience of sadness so poignant and important. It was not just the one incident of his parents' snub that worked on the man born blind. This was only the most recent of many times he had experienced rejection and silent scorn. It was not just one day's pressure put on him to toe the line under threat of exclusion. This was just the last of a long series of people strongly urging him to declare himself a worthless sinner who can no more think with his own head than he can see with his own eyes.

Every human has his or her own pools of sadness, remembered hurts, temptations to surrender to group pressure in order not to be "kicked out of (one's own version of) the synagogue."

For this reason it is most important to cultivate the attitudes so well displayed by the man born blind. Balance Humor — it is the last name that gives the first. Sense of humor is the human faculty that sees the incongruity of things. The mind knows what is the expected thing, the right thing. (For instance, a well-dressed, self-important man should be in control when he walks down the street.) Then the mind apprehends what incongruously surprising things sometimes show up. (This man slips, bottom-first, into a mud puddle.) Humor gives a kind of distance to events. A person seeing the humor of a situation can disentangle himself from things that are out of his control. In this way he can still be in control of himself.

St. Augustine links the beatitude "Blessed are they who mourn" with the faculty called sense of humor. At first glance, they seem to be strange bedfellows. But both mournfulness and humor see the rift between what should be and what is. Concerning important things that one cannot control, the appropriate thing to do is mourn. (Recall Jesus weeping over Jerusalem because he was not accepted by his own people, and, perhaps, Balance Humor feeling very sad because his parents refused to rejoice over their son's cure.)

Concerning the more trivial things one cannot control (like the illogical frenzy of the Pharisees) the appropriate thing to do is to refrain from letting one experience stir all the pools of remembered injustices. It is to see the humor of the present incongruity. "What fools these mortals be."

The challenge is to know which response is appropriate to which occasion. Most people all too quickly engage themselves in the spirit of mournfulness. Mourning has such a force to it that, whatever is mourned for, it can take over the person entirely. When this happens, there is no energy left. Jesus mourned over Jerusalem, but unacceptance did not swallow him up. Balance Humor mourned his parents' insensitivity, but he was not crushed by it. There were things he had to do, but one thing especially: find out more about the prophet from Galilee who had cured him.

Humor has a way of taking the sting out of a sad situation. If the man born blind were less of a person, the third degree he was put through would have been the last straw. He would have drowned in his pool of worthlessness. He would have said, "That's it! They are right. The one day I should be happy, I am made unhappy. My family wants nothing to do with me. The Pharisees are convinced that the man who cured me is a fraud. I'm a sinner, always have been. It was a sinner who gave me sight. I'll just go along with everybody else and admit I never did amount to anything... and never will!"

The man never spoke like that. Incongruity was on the other people's side. Humor was on his. He knew what had happened to him. No pressure would make him give it up. The others should have acknowledged Jesus to be a man sent by God to do God's purposes. They did not do so. Instead, they stumbled all over their own words; they even stooped to vituperation. The joke was on them. Balance Humor could not change them. And he would not let them change him. He did not fall into the mood of self-pity just because others were blind to the significance of why he was blind no longer.

He kept his humor. By doing so, he kept his balance. These both led him to perfect worship of our Lord.

Prayer of Balance Humor Within

Jesus, my Lord,
    distance me from superstition
    and from that quicksand of my drowning terror
    which is a touchiness
    that turns one hurt
    into the whole sum of all past hurts.
Don't let me corner God, your Father,
    so that I think of him as cause of all my rotten luck.

Sometimes I'm blind
   so that I may grope, darkly, to true vision.
Sometimes I'm sick, or out of sorts,
   so that I may be turned to your source-curing;
   or else, remembering mortality,
   hope for your promises of life beyond my power.

Let me remember this.
Not every evil — mine or other people's —
   is sent by you as curse.
And once I know your good,
   let me know it in an unforgetting way,
   as did the man born blind.
I, too, have people in my world
   who want me to be part of their bland culture.
They do not want to rock the boat or risk their world.
They think of me and my enthusiasms
   mostly as an inconvenience.
I can be so saddened by their snubs.
(It is my quicksand into deep pools of grief.)
Keep me from falling, Lord.
Keep me detached from things I can't control.

Let me mourn unrighted wrongs when it's appropriate.
But mostly, let me use good humor
   to give me gentle ways of understanding
   my flawed foolishness
   and other people's blunders, too.
This way I won't be swallowed up.
My mind and heart will be with you;
and present shocks of sadness
   will then take their rightful place — no more —
   as just one episode of incongruity:
      watched over by a God who gives me
      vision into all events
      and courage about truth
      and humor about baseness
      and balance to myself
      ...and wisdom not to worship pressure groups,
      but only you, you only.

Amen.

8

Bar None, Friend of Bar Timaeus

As they left Jericho a large crowd followed him. Now there were two blind men sitting at the side of the road. When they heard that it was Jesus who was passing by, they shouted, "Lord, Son of David, have pity on us!" And the crowd scolded them and told them to keep quiet, but they only shouted more loudly, "Lord, Son of David, have pity on us!"

Jesus stopped, called them over and said, "What do you want me to do for you?" They said to him, "Lord, let us have our sight back." Jesus felt pity for them and touched their eyes... and said, "Receive your sight. Your faith has saved you."

And immediately their sight returned and they followed him up the road.

Matthew 20:29-34; Mark 10:46-52
Luke 18:35-43

Mr. Bentback

Now at the Sheep Pool in Jerusalem there is a building... consisting of five porticos; and under these were crowds of sick people — blind, lame, paralyzed — waiting for the water to move, for at intervals the angel of the Lord came down into the pool, and the water was disturbed, and the first person to enter the water after this disturbance was cured of any ailment he suffered from. One man there had an illness which had lasted thirty-eight years, and when Jesus saw him lying there and knew he had been in this condition for a long time, he said, "Do you want to be well again?"

"Sir," the sick man replied, "I have no one to put me into the pool when the water is disturbed; and while I am still on the way, someone else gets there before me."

Jesus said, "Get up, pick up your sleeping mat and walk." The man was cured at once, and he picked up his mat and walked away.

Now the day happened to be the sabbath, so the Jews said to the man who had been cured, "It is the sabbath; you are not allowed to carry your sleeping-mat." He replied, "But the man who cured me told me, 'Pick up your mat and walk'." They asked, "Who is the man who said to you, 'Pick up your mat and walk'?" The man had no idea who it was. . . .

After a while Jesus met him in the Temple and said, "Now you are well again, but be sure not to sin any more, or something worse may happen to you."

John 5:2-14

As both St. Mark and St. Luke tell their story, there was only one blind beggar on the road going from Jericho to Jerusalem. Bar Timaeus was his name. St. Mark not only gives the name but also explains that it means "Bar (son of) Timaeus." He must have become a prominent member of the early Church. He surely was a disciple. Mark's concluding words are: "Immediately he received his sight and started to follow him up the road."

At the end of the road was Calvary. Doubtless, the Son of Timaeus continued to be with the close-knit group of men and women mentioned in the Acts of the Apostles. Otherwise Mark would not have gone to the trouble of making sure he stood out.

All three Evangelists stress the importance of this event. It was the very last miracle before Jesus began the final acts of salvation. The Gospels begin the accounts of Holy Week right after this episode.

It was as if Jesus meant to highlight the fact that true vision is the most important quality or ability we have. If we remain spiritually blind, perceiving things only from immediate sense-responses, we will miss the whole point of Christ's death. We will see it as a scandalous waste of a good man. We will judge the crucifixion as proof that God was unable to withstand the world's tendency toward vengeance and selfishness. We will assume that for all practical purposes God is dead. Only when the eyes-of-the-mind are opened to a spiritual understanding of what sin is, and to what love must do to win sinners over, only then can we understand why God would unconditionally love us to such a depth of passion.

The healing of Bar Timaeus' blindness was the sign, the final sign, of the healing that must take place in every person who would but dimly perceive the significance of Christ's love and the responsibility to be completely taken up by it.

Bar Timaeus was well remembered. He was like the last man up in the World Series who scores the winning run. He was the model in the early Church of all who must be healed by faith in order to understand the Gospel rightly.

According to Matthew, however, Bar Timaeus had a friend, also a blind beggar, who was right beside him. He shouted just as loudly. The crowd tried to repress him just as much. He was cured no less than his friend. All three synoptic Gospels speak of the very same incident. Yet Matthew remembers that there were two of them; Mark and Luke only mention Bar Timaeus, the more important.

I have given this friend the name "Bar None." This is to indicate that, unlike his friend who was the Son of Timaeus, he seems to have been the son of nobody important enough to be recalled.

I have given him that name, also, to indicate that "none could bar him" — he would not be deterred. Nobody could stop him from approaching Jesus to ask to be cured. Although many people tried, they were not able to scold him into silence.

It is fascinating that even in our Lord's time there was so much scolding going on. On one occasion, the Apostles scolded some parents who were asking Jesus to bless their children. Our Lord reprimanded his Twelve severely. "Let them come to me," he demanded, "and do not hinder them" (Mark 10:13-16). The Pharisees were forever scolding people who had the nerve to let themselves be healed on the Sabbath. Jesus, for his part, was forever unperturbed; he constantly insisted that people be brought to him.

This time, it was the crowd who took the role of spoil-sport. "When (the blind beggars) heard that it was Jesus who was passing by, they shouted, 'Lord, Son of David, have pity on us!' And the crowd scolded them and told them to keep quiet... but they shouted all the louder..."

Good for them! So many people, even today, keep trying to hinder others from approaching Jesus. Many do so because they have naturally sour dispositions . . . and they think God ought to be just as irritated by interruptions as they are. Others (the more efficient type, those leaning toward "perfectionism") have as rigid and as ruthless a schedule for Jesus as they have for themselves and cannot endure any frittering away of energy. They cannot imagine why God would want to waste his time on (those whom they consider to be) nobodies. Still others have that superstitious image of God as a person powerful in the way that wordly rulers are. They are forever telling others — especially those who are younger, or older, or in any way they consider inferior to them — that this Very Important Person (God) has too many momentous concerns than to be "bothering with the likes of you!"

It seems that scolders are always trying to keep people away from Jesus . . . and Jesus is always scolding the scolders, insisting that no one be hindered from his loving care.

Such was the case in this incident. "Call them to me," Jesus demanded. Right away, those busybodies changed their tune: "Get up, Jesus is calling for you. You having nothing to fear." I can imagine the beggars muttering "thanks a lot" (perhaps sarcastically) as they dusted themselves off. They were just pushed away by the crowd, maybe pushed down into the gutter as well; now they were slapped on the back by the same people who had just bullied them.

No matter. The crowd's fickleness did not make them fickle. They knew their need. They knew, by faith, that Jesus could do something about their neediness. They were very much alive to the presence of our Lord. Jesus gave them the opportunity to respond in whatever way they wished to. "What do you want me to do for you?" he asked them.

Surprisingly, their answer was direct. No beating around the bush. No extraneous matters mentioned. No hemming or hawing. No roll-call of past grievances. No complaints about other people. No statements like: "Well, for one thing, Lord, I wish you'd tell the crowd to quit picking on us. They've been doing that to us all our lives, making fun of us, too, just because we're blind. They take advantage of us, push us into ditches. Tell them to stop it!"

Nothing like that. All attention was focused on their own blindness and Jesus' power to heal them. "Lord," they said, "we want to see." And it was done, as simply and directly as it was asked for. The beggars then were praised for their faith. Jesus never missed an opportunity to affirm people for their goodness. This was an occasion for him to do so easily. They were men after his own heart.

Their faith-response was praiseworthy . . . and surprising. Jesus did not meet many who were as straightforward as they were. He did meet some — the unnamed people of this book are some of them — but he did not meet many. It would seem that he has not met too many since.

Most people act more like another unnamed person in the Gospel, whose story is told in St. John's Gospel (5:1-15). I have given him the name "Mr. Bentback," not because of his physical ailment, but because his mind kept bending back to all that was wrong in life. Although he had healthy eyes, he couldn't even see the Person who was trying to help him. He was so sick in his own disconsolate self-pity, nothing could get through to him. If the unnamed beggar could be called "Bar None," this character would be called "Bar Everybody." In his estimate of the situation, the whole world was conspiring to impede his happiness.

He had been lame for thirty-eight years. St. John remembers that Jesus "knew he had been so for a long time." The man was one of the many sick people who idled their time near one of the open pools of Jerusalem. Apparently, healings took place there when new water from some mountain aqueduct freshened the pool. It seems that only the first arrival in the pool was favored. The image one gets is that of throwing a few pieces of popcorn to pigeons in the park; some are lucky (or bullies), others have to wait until next time.

Jesus asked the man a simple question: "Do you want to be healed?" It was more a leading question than the one he asked the two blind beggars. He asked them, "What do you want me to do for you?" Here, our Lord put the word *healing* right to the man. What in the world could persuade anyone from not saying: "O, Wow, I sure do!" A simple yes would have been sufficient...any expression, as long as it was affirmative. All the man had to do was to agree to Jesus' offer.

He didn't. Our Lord asked him if he wanted to be healed. The man immediately went into a tirade of why he couldn't be: "Every time I get a chance, somebody else beats me to it!" This sounds like a broken record spoken by an old grouch. He probably made the same complaint, every day, until he knew it by heart: "Other people have friends who carry them right down to the pool at healing time. I have nobody who cares about me. These young folks elbow their way right past me. They don't care about how they crash the line and leave me miserable all these years!"

Jesus was still present. He patiently waded through this torrent of abusive words about how abusive other people were. He graciously disregarded the man's disregard of him. He healed Mr. Bentback anyway: "Get up, pick up your sleeping-mat and walk."

The Pharisees, naturally, were right on the spot. They complained, predictably, about such manual work on the Sabbath — someone carrying his mattress home on the day of rest. They made inquiries, but quickly closed the case. This man was so intensely into his own bitterness about how awful people were that he didn't even notice the Person who had cured him.

Later on that afternoon, they met again. Jesus did not praise this man for his faith. He had no faith. He was too preoccupied with his own misery. He was bent on proving how unjustly he had been treated. Instead of praising him, Jesus gave him a warning: "Now that you are well, be sure not to sin again, or something worse will happen to you."

The man was not straight: he was bent over, and bent back (mentally) upon himself, impenetrable to grace. That's the way grouchy people get. They are so intent upon their own misfortune, and so angry about those who have made them so, they cannot see any fresh possibilities; they are not open to any good that might be available to them.

Jesus is not able to praise this kind of individual. He can only heal them and hope they will stop being so grouchy. On the other hand, Jesus generously praised the faith of Bar Timaeus and his friend. They knew what they needed, refused to let busybodies stop them, asked for help without equivocation, received their sight...and stayed to learn the full import of their new vision, as they "started to follow Jesus up the road."

There is a time-honored phrase called "distractions in prayer" which can best explain my suggestion that the lame man's response to Jesus was not surprising, while the response of the two blind beggars was surprising.

Most people admit that they get distracted when they try to pray. Distraction is precisely what the lame man in St. John's Gospel had. Distraction has its source in the agitated memory. We cannot seem to stop the habit of thinking about miseries previously endured. It could be a physical misfortune, like the lame man's. It could be other people who have treated us unfairly. We still suffer from the memory of how we were cheated out of our inheritance, or were less favored by parents, or wronged on the job, or villified by gossips, or not spoken to by others, or ill-treated by a friend (or who we *thought* was a friend).

The lame man in the Gospel was elbowed out of the way by those who could hustle better than he. It wasn't fair; injustices never are. But he didn't have to keep rubbing the wounds of his hurt so hard that he was unable to be actually present to what God wanted to do for him. He didn't *have to* be so distracted by his own right to feel bad, which he so testily insisted on. He did, though.
We do, too, sometimes.
The other source of distraction, besides the agitated memory, is the imagination. Our brains do more than bend back upon time gone by, uselessly reliving the hurt that happened in the unchangeable past. This is bad enough. But we also add anxiety about the future to the misery of old remembrances. Imagination triggers woe upon woe and then it worries the worst possible alternative into existence as though it were happening already. Imagination bases its anxiety upon grievances stored up by the fault-finding memory: "Nobody has cared about me yet; nobody will tomorrow!...I've been a failure so far; things will never change, so why try!...I never got any good breaks before; isn't it awful about how the world is going nowadays!"
The lame man couldn't hear what Jesus was saying: "Do you want to be healed? Do you want to be happy?" He could only run on and on with the same litany of sorrows that he always spoke; he could only look forward to the same unhappiness that he always had. Prayer — and faith that feeds it — was blocked out from him because he was bent back on himself.
We all have to some extent this strong tendency to fall into our own shell of self-pity. We had better be advised of its danger and determine not to be powerless before it.
Let the antics of the lame man serve as warning. Let the simple faith of the two blind beggars serve as model. The one character could not pray because of hurts that refused to be forgotten. The two blind men were just as beggarly, just as maltreated as he. Yet, somehow, even in their blindness, they could see things more clearly. The hurts and heedlessness they suffered did not stop them from realizing what was going on right then and there. They were alert to the moment at hand. They were not distracted. When Jesus asked them, "What do you want?" they responded in a way that made sense. Our Lord was someone *real* to them.
Jesus asks the same of us: "What do you want? What do you want me to do for you? What wisdom do you want me to give you? What fresh hope can I grace you with? What new insights, new approaches, can I steer your way? How do you want me to be with you?"
When Jesus begins his prayer with us in any of these ways, we had

better acknowledge who it is who asks for our response. It would be well to pray for the spirit of the last two men Jesus cured. Pray for the spirit that can wade right through the busybody bystanders from without and the busybody distractions from within, and say to Jesus, as honestly as we can: "My Lord, I want you to help me see."

Prayer of Mr. Bar None Within

Jesus, my Lord,
   help me to un-mob myself
      so that I may be more present to your care.
I have so many things to do,
     so many urgencies,
       such a long, fatiguing list of reasons
         why I can't take time to pray.
They are like voices, a whole mob of voices,
     telling me not to slow down,
     warning me not to waste your time,
     scolding me into feverish activity.
Give me the spirit of the two blind beggars
     whose faith you praised so graciously.
Don't let my busy-ness
     become a bunch of busybodies
     trying to hinder me from hearing you.

And help me squelch
     that mob-scene in my own mind, too.
The wrongs I've suffered, the unfair treatment,
     the bitterly recalled injustices and snubs...
     these are the worst of scoldings:
     I keep thinking of them and thinking of them,
     turning and turning on the same old hurts,
     constantly scolding those who have scolded me
     'til I become a scold myself,
     no less ill-tempered than that old grouch
     who wouldn't let you get a word in edgewise.
Let me be not so busy with the memory
     of all these unrequited wrongs.

They are a mob of thoughts
    who try to hinder me
    from letting you be with me.

I know you love me.
You want to speak to me and make me whole.
You want to seek out my response,
    my lively, here-and-now response.
Let me be straight with you,
    unbent by the crowd's badgering
    (especially the crowd inside my head).

Although I'm blind and cannot see you clearly,
I do have faith enough to feel your presence;
And I do know that you ask me,
    as surely as you've asked all other beggars born before me:
    "What do you want me to do for you?"
    "What is it you want me to be for you?"

Let me be alert enough to tell you, clearly.

Amen.

9

Shy Limedark

Now there was a woman suffering from a hemorrhage for twelve years, whom no one had been able to cure. She came up behind...Jesus...and touched his cloak. "If I can touch even his clothes," she told herself, "I shall be well again." And the source of her bleeding dried up instantly, and she felt in herself that she was cured of her complaint.

Jesus turned round in the crowd and said, "Who touched me?" When they all denied that they had, Peter and his companions said, "Master, it is the crowds round you, pushing." But Jesus said, "Somebody touched me. I felt that power had gone out from me."

Seeing herself discovered, the woman came forward trembling and falling at his feet explained in front of all the people why she had touched him and how she had been cured at that very moment. "My daughter," he said, "your faith has restored you to health; go in peace."

Luke 8:43-48; Mark 5:25-34
Matthew 9:20-22

*T*his woman is usually given the title "the woman with the flow of blood." Shyness was her personality trait. Faith was her saving grace.

Shy, very shy. She showed this representative quality so perfectly, it is most fitting that we give her this name somehow. We don't know whether she was Miss or Mrs.; and the designation Ms. ill befits her. Even today, she'd be the last woman in the world to write Ms. before her name. It would be wrong to call her "Madam Shy," or "Her Shyness," for this would indicate a regal bearing, a forthright individual who would be comfortable at the headtable of any gathering.

Such was hardly the case. Her outstanding quality was that she did not want to stand out. The one thing conspicuous about her was that she wanted to be inconspicuous. The cause may have been embarrassment about her malady. It may also have been part of her natural deference, her wanting to remain unmasked in the sea of anonymity, her dread of being put on the spot under any conditions.

She did not like the limelight; indeed, she shied away from it. Of all the unnamed people in the Gospel, it's safe to say that she is the person who would rather stay unnamed. Even so — even at the risk of causing her displeasure — I will give her the first name "Shy" and the last name "Limedark." These names indicate her prevalent attitude and her preferred atmosphere.

Shy Limedark had suffered for a long time. All three Gospels agree that it was twelve years. It seems to have been a serious and prolonged kind of menstrual bleeding which weakened her, pained her, and doubtless caused her no little embarrassment. St. Luke reports that she had done her human best to improve her situation, but she did not improve. St. Mark, far less loyal to the medical profession (and perhaps a bit embittered by some personal experience of his own) adds that she "suffered much at the hands of many physicians...and found no benefit, but rather grew worse."

Whichever Evangelist was more correct in this detail, one thing is certain — she was very, very discouraged. She was at her wit's end. The only hope left was to hope in a miracle from God. Jesus was a prophet of God. He had already cured many people with marvelous suddenness and with his own declaration that his healing power had come from his Father, the one and only God.

She believed this. Her faith was never doubted, not by Jesus, not by the Evangelists, not by herself. She had no trouble believing that the miracle would happen; she just wanted the miracle to be worked her way. Nothing splashy. No awestruck bystanders to buzz to all their neighbors afterward about the big event. No limelight. A nice, simple, unadorned, liturgy of cure. Just "me and Jesus."

It did not work out that way. It seldom does, with anybody. Jesus does answer our prayers, always. Sometimes he says, "No (or Wait)"; sometimes he says, "Yes, I will." But when he says "Yes," it rarely happens as we wanted it to happen. The "how" of it is in God's hands, and God is a master of the unexpected. Jesus grants us the *fact* of healing; he surprises us about the *form* of it.

Such was the case with Shy Limedark. St. Mark describes the fact, the inward reality: "She touched the hem of his garment and at once the flow of her blood was stopped, and she felt in her body that she was healed of her affliction." That was it. At last, her prayers were answered. At this point, we can infer that she was about to slink away. Doubtless, she would have spent hours and hours praying her prayers of gratitude in the privacy of her own room or in the most inconspicuous place in the synagogue.

But the luxury of "no fuss over me" was not granted her. "Who touched me?" Jesus called out loud, in a commanding voice that hushed and stilled the crowd. Peter suggested that this was a foolish question. There were so many milling around, jostling one another, and Jesus, too. Who could distinguish one touch from another?

Jesus waited. He wanted Shy Limedark to assert herself. The "closed door, secret chamber" kind of piety was not enough in this case. Our Lord selected the most demure, uneffacing person he came across and "put her on stage," demanding that she proclaim her faith loudly...from the housetops. St. Luke records this part of it, most beautifully. "The woman, seeing that *she had not escaped notice*, came up trembling...and declared *in the presence of all the people* why she had touched him and how she had been healed instantly."

I wonder what happened to her afterward. Was she cured of her shyness as well as her twelve-year hemorrhage? I don't think that she had a reversal of personality, that she turned into an articulate witness to her faith like Judith or St. Joan of Arc. She was not that type. But I think she probably did share more of herself with others than she did before. Less self-consciously, she let other people see and learn from the faith she had within herself. When occasions arose, she did not shy away from speaking her version of Mary's Magnificat — "I have made God great by letting him prove his goodness to me" — and I am sure that the many people who heard her praise God out loud marvelled...and were moved to pray much better.

Regardless of where we would place ourselves on the scale of extrovert-introvert, there is a bit of Shy Limedark in us all. We could seem to be the most outgoing of people, self-expressive to the point of translucence, self-evident almost to the point of exhibitionism, a veritable showcase with a flair for the floodlights. Yet there are patches in this self-display which we prefer to keep secret even from ourselves.

Our guarded diffidence may only be indirectly religious. "Unwillingness to open up" may be related not so much to God as to others. Spouse may never tell spouse what irritating habits are feeding a resentment, until it is too late. Friend may never tell friend what the fear is or what the real wants are, until the friendship is dissolved, or rather, erodes for lack of roots strong enough to withstand the storms of thoughtlessness when they finally do come.

Children won't tell their parents about the high hopes and low misgivings that they have. Why? I don't know. Everyone is different: fear of being shouted at, or preached to, or treated with shocked surprise or (worst of all) indifference. Whatever the reason, the general attitude is shyness, a certain dreading of the limelight, a reticence, a refusing to be observed. ("Where did you go?" "Out." "What did you do?" "Nothing.'")

Parents relating to their children and adults relating to younger people have their own areas of diffidence, almost miserliness with words. Oh, of their successes and their favorite anecdotes of failures, there is no end of reruns ("When I was a boy, I walked to school and had it tough!" "I want you to get an education and not make the mistake I made in life!") But how we managed through the secret horrors that we had, the terrifying self-doubts that plagued us, our loneliness, temptations, sometimes fruitless labors, how we lived with our experience of prayer when God seemed close and we felt right, when love of a friend or teacher quickened our hearts to new worlds of possibility and larger hopes — these personal, deep-felt things are often meagerly dispensed. And so the adolescent is shortchanged because self-revelation of either the worst or the best in us is too embarrassing to be brought up.

It is often a fault. I am not recommending the other extreme — to constantly wear one's heart on one's sleeve, or give an on-the-spot report of every irritating habit a friend has, or declaim at length one's spiritual autobiography — when the youngster just wants directions to the drugstore. But there are times when we, like Shy Limedark, really would rather stay unnoticed, when the better thing would be to come right out in the open and "declare in the presence of all the people involved" just who we are and how we got that way and what we really want.

The same holds even more forcefully with what relates directly to one's faith. Many people manifest a formidable guardedness about their prayer life and their personal growth in faith.

Oh, there are exceptions. There are some people who talk non-stop about their spiritual healing. They go on and on about their love for God until it almost seems that their faith is a club by which they disdainfully put down the lesser gifted.

But these rare cases cannot blur the work of the Holy Spirit these last twenty years or so. Lately, the world has witnessed a marvelous revival of public testimonies to faith. Houses of prayer have mushroomed, as well as charismatic meetings and all manner of assemblies where faith-sharing can take place. It is as if the whole world yearns for an atmosphere where God can be talked about and thanked without embarrassment. The hearts of humans groan for an environment where we will not be stifled by the cultural demand that we speak only about gossip and sports and sex and politics and causes for resentment, reasons why we get tired, and the latest weather report.

The Holy Spirit yearns to do what Jesus did with Shy Limedark, to bring us out of our reluctance to speak about God and our personal prayer. And even though we tremble with self-consciousness and words don't always come out right, we are to proclaim how we have made contact with our Lord, and how this contact has made a difference in our lives.

Prayer of Shy Limedark Within

Jesus, my Lord,
    put a little more power in my pushlessness.

I have a certain shyness, strangely secret even to myself.
Sometimes I'm an open book, easy to understand;
Sometimes I'm reticent when I know it's right to be so:
    when prudence dictates going to my room alone
    and praying in secret to my Father, as you taught me.

But sometimes there's those in-between concerns
    and sometimes I'm afraid to say just what I feel
    and where the feeling-sources are

and how they got that way...
when it would be better if I had been a bit more obvious
to others and myself.
And there are times when I prefer to cringe away from crowds
and to avoid an open statement of my loyalty to you
(when people might make fun of me for it
or when they might make more of it
than I think I can handle).

I so often want to be in control of everything
— everything neat and "no fuss" —
like the woman in the Gospel.
Draw me out, Lord;
Don't let me fear the risk
of not expressing myself exactly as I'd like to,
of being laughed at,
of being asked more questions than I'd like,
or whatever else the reasons are that cause me to be shy.

Draw me out, as you did Shy Limedark,
into the spotlight of self-revelation.
Let me not fear to speak my praise of you,
my love for you,
my ways in which your ways of touching me
have made God great.

Let me do this, so that, by speaking up
you can tell me
with words that will be obvious to all,
that faith has saved me,
that I may go in peace.

Amen.

10

Ms. Familiarity

Jesus, tired by the journey, sat down by the well. It was about noon. When a Samaritan woman came to draw water, Jesus said to her, "Give me a drink." ... The Samaritan woman said to him, "What? You are a Jew and you ask me, a Samaritan, for a drink?" Jews do not associate with Samaritans. Jesus replied:
> "If you only knew what God is offering...
> you would have been the one to ask,
> and he would have given you living water."

"You have no bucket, sir," she answered, "and the well is deep; how could you get this living water? Are you greater than our father Jacob......?" Jesus replied:
> "Whoever drinks this water
> will get thirsty again;
> but anyone who drinks the water that I shall give
> will never be thirsty again;
> the water that I shall give
> will turn into a spring inside him,
> welling up to eternal life."

"Sir," said the woman, "give me some of that water, so that I may never get thirsty and never have to come here again to draw water." "Go and call your husband," he said to her, "and come back here." The woman answered, "I have no husband." He said to her, "You are right to say, 'I have no husband'; for although you have had five, the one you have now is not your husband. You spoke the truth there." "I see you are a prophet, sir," said the woman... Jesus said:
> "...God is spirit,
> and those who worship
> must worship in spirit and truth."

The woman said to him, "I know that Christ is coming; and when he comes, he will tell us everything." Jesus said, "I who am speaking to you, I am he."
... The woman put down her water jar and hurried back to the town to tell the people, "Come and see a man who has told me everything I ever did. I wonder if he is the Christ?" This brought people out of the town and they started walking towards him. . .

Many Samaritans of that town had believed in him on the strength of the woman's testimony when she said, "He told me all I have ever done." So, when the Samaritans came up to him, they begged him to stay with them. He stayed for two days, and when he spoke to them many more came to believe; and they said to the woman, "Now we no longer believe because of what you told us; we have heard him ourselves and we know that he really is the savior of the world."

John 4:5-42

This chapter is a sister-piece to the one before. The woman by the well in Samaria could be, in spirit, sister to the woman who was healed of her passage of blood. They were very different from each other, as sisters often are. The woman cured of her hemorrhage was uncomfortably shy; she preferred not to express herself, avoiding social interchange as much as possible. The woman by the well was, on the contrary, quite comfortable with social interchange, even with strangers, even with those people whom custom labeled as taboo. Far from being shy, this woman could banter with the best of them.

Perhaps it came from so much practice. She had already gone through five husbands. We know she was living with a sixth, not her husband. It does not seem that she was a "woman of the streets;" she was a shade above such disrespectability. But she was a "woman of the world." Conversation was not difficult for her. Hardly anything could put her at a loss for words. Occasions that would cause another person to be shocked, or stunned into silence, only served to whet her curiosity and start her talking in that half-teasing, easy-going, hail-stranger-well-met way of hers.

I have given her the name "Ms. Familiarity" for a number of reasons. She certainly did not want to be labeled either Miss or Mrs. — her marital status was the one thing she was secretive about. Ms. seems as right for her as it was wrong for her "sister" in the last story.

And the name "Familiarity" expresses (to me at least) the major chord of her character. I use that word in both the good and bad sense. It was not hard to get words or ideas out of her. She was an interesting person and interested in others. She readily adapted to new swings of the conversation. We don't know whether she was fun-loving or not, but chances are she was. She was a pleaser. Had she lived today, she'd be perfect as an interviewer on a television talk-show. Her breezy familiarity provided Jesus with the best opportunity to probe deeper and deeper into the universal purpose and spiritual meaning of his mission.

The woman was also "Familiarity" in the bad sense. As is so often the case with outgoing people, she tended to be shallow. Her preference was to keep things light. There is a sadness within her jocular repartee which she was probably not aware of. A pleaser keeps running on the track of pleasing even when something within can sense misgivings and deep melancholy. The promptings of the heart are resisted. Almost in a panic of escape, the void of self-doubt becomes filled with words, frothy words, familiar ways of bouncing back and forth with people, breeziness that breezes by all urgencies to stop, and think, and pray.

It is interesting that Jesus approached these two "sisters" in completely different ways. The shy introvert who recoiled from the floodlights he forced to speak up. He cured her *physical* wounds so that she would courageously proclaim his mercy. The bold extrovert who was seldom at a loss for words Jesus forced to quiet down. He cured her *psychological* ailment. He broke down all those "barriers of bantering" she had erected so that she would not have to think about how and why she was living her life, and where was her life going.

Jesus slowed her down and got her thinking. This, too, was a miracle — different from the other — just the right one for her.

She seemed to be so relieved. At last, she did not have to fake it. She could get off that carousel of words and works and postures and social graces. She was found out. This Prophet from Galilee had discovered depths in her. He seriously addressed them and called her to her sins...and senses. He invited her to drink of the waters of grace that would quench her thirst forever and let her discontinue her frantic pursuit of keeping up a good front.

I can see the wrinkles of her brow smooth out, the fixed smile loosen, the flippant words die off, the somewhat taunting expression of her eyes subside. Work was going on inwardly, at last. Jesus understood, as no one had before, that she had depth in her. He knew the pain and hurt she had covered up so successfully, until he met her. From that time on she could live in depth. She need no longer pose with antic superficiality, with pantomimes of pleasantries. At last!

Then quickly, not caring whether she would or would not be believed, she went to her villagers and told them of the miracle, *her* kind of miracle: "He told me all that I have ever done."

She cared not how she would be received. Respectable people probably disliked her; maybe feared her. Certainly, she was not one of their set. Gossips would have known part of her sordid past. Even good-natured neighbors were probably concerned about her brazen ways. If familiarity breeds contempt, her name is rightly given from this aspect, too.

The villagers did believe her story. They went to see our Lord and stayed with him for two whole days. Even so, there is a note of put-down in their last remark to her. Instead of thanking the person who initiated their beautiful weekend retreat, they told her: "We no longer believe because of what you have said, for we have heard ourselves and we know that this is in truth the savior of the world."

Surely this is one of St. John's favorite theological points, that Jesus is to be known by a personally experienced faith-contact, not just by hearsay. Even so, by the very abrupt way they put their statement, one still can feel the contempt with which they wrote her off.

No matter. It may have hurt, but it didn't really matter. She announced the good news and let Jesus take it from there. She was a different person; she was a woman of stillness, a person of purpose, a drinker of the deep thirst-quenching waters of eternal life.

The behavioral tendency that I have sketched and attributed to Ms. Familiarity is one we all have, one way or another.

We all have a hobby-horse or two that we ride to death: cars, sports, the job, the neighbors, a favorite arena of politics, a certain kind of music, a cluster of favorite jokes, or stories about the good old days...whatever. We also have a certain manner of swinging along the conversation, keeping it bright, and sometimes brittle, having our way with pleasantries to show that we are people of the world.

Not all of this is bad, of course; lightness-of-touch, tact, delicacy, prudent considerations of time and place are comfortable qualities, when exercised appropriately. We can't always be deep philosophers, intensely probing the depths of our souls.

But sometimes the tendency to stick with familiar subjects, in a mood of familiarity, is definitely inappropriate. It becomes an escape from the discipline of thought. It turns into social games by which people play off one another and prevent self from being still long enough to wonder about those truths which, like wells, are very deep and silent.

It is at these times that we need the positive qualities of the woman of Samaria. When Jesus brought her up short, broke off her games, saw through the easy-going surface to the sores beneath, she did not stop the process. She did not argue or dismiss with another joke this challenge to think more deeply about herself. She stayed with it. By doing so, she gradually saw the truth that set her free.

Such grace can be our grace too, when we let it happen. When someone cuts through our superficial mannerisms and speaks of our deep hurts within, deep sins we're scared to think of, deep thoughts we've starved with inattentiveness . . . when this takes place, it is a call to slow down to a stop. Reflect. Take stock. Consider slowly, sacredly, the possible truth of what was revealed.

It is better if such a someone is kind, speaking without bitterness, as Jesus spoke to the woman at the well. But even if said unkindly, the truth will still be true. It may be just what we need to deepen down and straighten out. Even if the truth hurts, it may come as a relief to us, a mental relief which gives a kind of healing.

Such was the case with Ms. Familiarity. We, too, can feel a certain sense of power and peace, once we've been jolted to our depths, and there discover that we do have depths, and need not be afraid of them any longer.

Prayer of Ms. Familiarity Within

Jesus my Lord,
    I do not expect you to visit me
    by any well or water fountain.
But I do see me inside that woman you did meet.
For I, too, get familiar, over-familiar, with you
    and with the words you've spoken.
I sometimes surface all too quickly with my own ideas.
I don't wait long enough to take you seriously;
    I try to maneuver you with questions,
    plays on words,
    familiar banterings . . .

Let me be more cautious, Lord.
Let me be more respectful.
The words you speak are life,
    like water that quenches deepest thirst.
Let me be patient with them,
    reverent, especially to those words
    that speak of things I want to escape from.

And let me be reverent toward those people and occasions
    you send my way:
    by which the games I play are broken down;
    by which I'm faced with challenges to grow,
    sins to be sorry for,
    hopes and ideals I try to hide away
    because they mean I'll have to work them through.

Let me be serious about the serious side of me.
And thank you always
    for the respect you grant me by these graces.
You honor me by helping me to understand my depth.
Also — whether others hold me in contempt or not —
    let me give praise and witness
    to the villagers of my inheritance:
For you've made known to me
    all I have ever done...or thought...in depth.

Amen.

11
Steward Wonder

Three days later there was a wedding at Cana in Galilee. The mother of Jesus was there, and Jesus and his disciples had also been invited. When they ran out of wine, since the wine provided for the wedding was all finished, the mother of Jesus said to him, "They have no wine." Jesus said, "Woman, why turn to me? My hour has not come yet."

His mother said to the servants, "Do whatever he tells you."

There were six stone water jars standing there, meant for the ablutions that are customary among the Jews; each could hold twenty or thirty gallons. Jesus said to the servants, "Fill the jars with water," and they filled them to the brim. "Draw some out now," he told them, "and take it to the steward."

They did this; the steward tasted the water, and it had turned into wine. Having no idea where it came from — only the servants who had drawn the water knew — the steward called the bridegroom and said, "People generally serve the best wine first, and keep the cheaper sort till the guests have had plenty to drink; but you have kept the best wine till now."

This was the first of the signs given by Jesus; it was given at Cana in Galilee. He let his glory be seen, and his disciples believed in him.

John 2:1-12

The name Steward is a rather common one, both personally and occupationally. The attribute that could give a person the name of Wonder is much more rare.

This is the way I would like to refer to the unnamed person who figured so prominently in St. John's account of the Wedding Feast at Cana. He was an ordinary individual, not very much a stranger for all the span of centuries that separate him from today's world. He is uncommon only in his admirable quality of wonder.

The main reason we say this about him is because of the way he turned to Mary, the Mother of Jesus, and paid close attention to how she managed things. No doubt, it was his respect for Mary that prompted him to be so thoughtful about her Son. Respect turned to thoughtfulness; thoughtfulness to wonder; wonder to devotion. This seems to be the sequence of his story.

According to John's Gospel, Jesus himself began his career with thoughtfulness. His first sign was an act of neighborly assistance for two families who would have been humiliated, if it hadn't been for his help.

There was a wedding feast at Cana. Mary was mentioned first. She certainly was invited. Probably the parents of bride and groom were close friends of hers. Then our Lord is mentioned: "And Jesus and his disciples had also been invited." Nobody knows how deliberate St. John was in this list of protocol. But "also invited" sounds something like "also ran." It could be that Jesus was asked to come because the wedding party wanted to make sure Mary would.

If this were the case, it would make the family drama all the more understandable and intense. Jesus had just returned to Galilee from the Jordan River. On the trip back, he had summoned at least four men to be his followers — Peter, Andrew, Philip, and Nathaniel (John 1:40-46). The other Evangelists would include at least two more; James and John are always spoken of as being together with Peter and Andrew. Right on the spot, they left what they were doing and followed him.

Three days afterward, they all went to the wedding. It is unlikely that the disciples (probably all twelve by then) were personally invited. They came along because they were friends of Jesus. I can hear the father of the bride saying, "Sure, by all means, let them come. They are welcome." I can also visualize him scratching his head and wondering if he ordered enough wine, now that unexpected guests had joined the party.

Peter and Company may very well have been the cause for the quick depletion of the wine cellar. Whatever the cause, the fact was

that the supply was diminishing. If it ran out — and it soon would —
the festivity would end in a disaster. Both families would be terribly
embarrassed. Young bride and groom would have seen their day of
joy turned into a day of bitter memories. Mary was the first to notice the shortage. She turned to Jesus and
said, in a voice loud enough to be overheard, "They have no wine."
It could not have been a simple statement of fact. Mother expected
Son to do something about it. Since there were no previous displays
of signs and miracles — no precedent established yet — I suppose
Mary thought Jesus would send one of his disciples off to procure
more wine from a local delicatessen or a friend. This would make
even more sense if Mary realized that it was Jesus' disciples who
were the main reason for the dangerously low supply.
Our Lord knew that his mother expected something from him. He
replied, in so many words: "You want me to do something. I am not
willing to. I am not ready to do it." His actual words were: "Woman,
why turn to me? My hour has not come yet."
To call one's mother "woman" was not insulting then, as it might
be in North America today. But it was a rather formal way for Jesus
to address his mother in such domestic circumstances. The designation "woman" was reserved for something like state occasions, like
the circumstances that gave rise to his statement made to Mary from
the cross.
Something was up, surely. Dramatic things were happening. Surprising things. Jesus was always so warm and approachable; now he
is formal, almost dignitary-like. Jesus was always so obedient; now
he refuses to grant his mother a simple request. Jesus was always so
understandable; now he speaks strangely and solemnly about some
destiny — an "hour" — that was coming.
The chief steward must have witnessed this peculiar dialogue. The
mere mention of wine running short would have demanded his
attention. Doubtless, he was already concerned about it. Doubtless
also, he would have been relieved to hear Mary ask her Son to take
care of the situation.
I imagine that amazement came over him when he heard Christ
reply the way he did. (Chief stewards of that time were not profes-
sional caterers hired for the evening. They were close friends of the
family. We have every reason to suppose that he was a friend of both
Jesus and Mary.)
The man was bewildered by the abrupt way the Son refused his
mother's simple request. He was even more amazed at the way this
refusal was expressed. "Oh, oh!" he may have thought, "Here

comes trouble. The wine is running out; and now there's going to be a big fight between two people I dearly love. Mary will probably turn on her heels and stalk home, muttering how wrong it was to be publicly insulted like that...and refused by her own son...when, after all, she was only trying to help those two families...and, after all, it was because of *his* friends that the wine ran out in the first place. Then everybody will be ill at ease. And the beautiful marriage feast will end up in a big flop. I don't blame Mary for being hurt. Why did Jesus say those things?"

The man may have whispered such things to himself. Whether he did or not, it is very likely that his sense of amazement soon turned into wonder. He marveled at the way Mary managed herself. She did *not* run away in a huff. She did *not* complain or show any kind of upset over her Son's response.

She was gentle, affable, thoughtful — oh, so thoughtful. Something in her eyes made the steward wonder even more. Mary understood that what sounded like a rebuff was not a rebuff. She looked around the room, got the servants' attention, called them over and told them, simply, "Do whatever he tells you."

Everyone seemed relieved. The party went about its business. The chief steward probably relaxed. Jesus would send the servants out to friends of his who had the means of refilling the wine jars.

The steward did not expect the next episode, which caused him further wonder. Six water jars were filled — altogether it amounted to 240 gallons! enough to satisfy the needs of many wedding feasts! Servants brought some of the liquid to the chief steward. It was his job to make sure all food and drink passed inspection. Marvel upon marvel: this lavish new supply was far better than the best in stock.

Perhaps the steward then understood why the exchange of words had to take place before the wondrous event could happen. This was the first of our Lord's signs: "It was given at Cana in Galilee. He let his glory be seen, *and his disciples believed in him.*"

What occurred at Cana was not only a miracle, helping out a couple in distress; it was a *sign*, an event that revealed the significance of who Jesus really was and what he came to do. It showed Christ's care for those in trouble, his blessing on the sacrament of marriage, his desire that people enjoy themselves at a celebration.

It was a sign of these things right away. It was also the inauguration sign of much, much more. It was the first of his many miracles of care; the initial display of undeniable authority over all created things; the beginning of his establishment of the New Covenant, which is as different from the Old Covenant as best wine is different from water.

"It was the first . . . and his disciples believed in him." That, after all, was the point of it. A sign is not a sign unless it is significant. It would not have been significant unless the disciples somehow were made to pay attention. We understand, after the fact, that the scene which seemed like an argument between Mother and Son was really Christ's way of making sure his action would be taken seriously. If the deed were less dramatically administered, it wouldn't have been noticed as much.

We understand it now . . . *after* the fact. The chief steward understood it, too. But it must have been a tense experience as the event unfolded, *before* all the pieces were put together.

The people at that wedding feast had nothing else to do but wait it out with uncomfortable concern, a certain empathy for Mary's seeming embarrassment, and a feeling of wonder, "What in the world will happen next?"

Mary didn't wonder, not in the way they did. She knew. Her influence on her Son was enough to speed up the schedule of his active career. She was serene in her directions of events. There were few words. We only hear two short phrases from her; and there is nothing to suggest that she had anything more to say. The first phrase spoke of her thoughtfulness: "They have no wine." The second spoke of her gentle guidance: "Do whatever he tells you."

She has never ceased saying the same two things. Cana of Galilee witnessed the first of her signs, too. All generations have relied on her thoughtfulness. All who are blessed with faith have experienced her quiet guidance, drawing our attention to her Son, telling us to do his will, urging us to stay calm until all the facts are in.

Steward Wonder was the first to witness Mary's significance. He is the pioneer of true devotion to the Mother of our Lord. He saw her kindness, knew her care for people in trouble, felt the power of her intercession, and praised her for the way it all worked out.

Amazement turned to wonder. Thanks to Mary, the steward was wonder-full.

In one way, there is no need to mention that we all have the "spirit of Steward Wonder" within us. Everyone who follows Christ must, of necessity, honor his mother. The love of them is so interwoven — it is so much of one piece, both in Scripture and in tradition — that we cannot neglect her any more than the bride and groom could invite Mary to Cana without inviting Jesus.

Devotion to Mary, therefore, is taken care of automatically by baptism. But just as the grace of baptism can shrivel into nothingness unless we cherish our unity with Christ, so can our link with his mother atrophy if we never give it the care of our attention.

We need Mary. We need the knowledge of her presence with us and the feeling of her maternal affection. We need her especially in those circumstances that could be likened to the experience at Cana of Galilee.

We, too, have had occasion to be puzzled by the ways of Christ. Injustices are committed and we wonder why Jesus doesn't step in and do something. Sometimes, people representing the Church even do these wrongs. They cause scandal or embarrassment... perhaps something like drinking too much wine at a wedding feast, or something more harmful.

We feel for the people hurt by these scandals. And we are shocked sometimes, because Jesus does not seem to care. We are tempted to do what the wedding party thought that Mary might do (but didn't) — go off in a huff, take Christ's words, "It's not my business" as the final answer, and abdicate our faith.

It is most important, at these times especially, that we pray to Mary. The time of prayer need not be filled with words. Better if it isn't. Let prayer be a simple sense of her presence, a mood of wonder, and a readiness to wait patiently for things to develop further.

Mary will not speak much with us. Hers is a presence that is almost wordless. We will somehow be aware of her thoughtfulness when our supplies run low; we will be conscious of the way she gently guides us to her Son; we will be instructed to do whatever he tells us to do. And then, at the time that Jesus has decided on, we will witness the signs of his power and love... and we will learn to believe in him more deeply.

The spirit of Steward Wonder can help us turn to Mary when the serious evils in the world bewilder us and cause us to doubt God's providence.

The same spirit can help us in other ways as well. We are tempted to turn not only from Jesus when it seems he has rebuffed us, but also from others when they do the same thing...for no apparent reason. We ask a friend to do a favor, and the friend doesn't do it, even though he's not all that busy. We have a date or luncheon appointment, and we are stood up, without any explanation. An ordinarily reliable person promises to deliver something by afternoon, and it never comes. We write three letters to a member of our family, and we never get a reply, not even a postcard...

These ordinary situations can pull us up short; they leave us feeling stranded. We are puzzled by the apparent bad will expressed by someone we expected better treatment from.

In these situations, too, it would be well to put on the spirit of the man who got his spirit from watching Mary manage things. Mary was pulled up short by Jesus' unexpected behavior. It "wasn't like him" to act that way. There must have been something else involved that she was not aware of. She would wait, and as she continued to wait, she renewed her confidence in the very Person who appeared to let her down. At the very time Jesus seemed to be so unreliable, she was telling the servants to trust him.

We don't know either why people sometimes let us down. Until we know for certain, let us wait in the same way. One failure to respond does not imply a total dissolution of all care and communication.

During our own versions of the wedding feast of Cana, let us be patient when people tell us, "No, I won't!" Let the unnamed steward of the Gospel point out Mary to us. Let Mary calm us down and wait it out with us. She will help us learn what to do while we are waiting.

Prayer of Steward Wonder Within

Jesus, my Lord,
    I don't have all the facts at my disposal.
I am not God.
I don't know why some people seem to change,
    people who were once my friends, fun to be with,
        dependable;
    and then abruptly turn their back on me.
    I don't know why they do so.

And neither do I know why you seem to do the same, sometimes.
You let such evil in the world continue.
You let so many be embarrassed by your ways
    because some of your followers cause scandals
    and people quickly think it's all your fault.
I don't know why these things should happen;
    or why you, sometimes —
    sometimes others —
        just don't seem to care.

Give me the grace to wait it out,
    not denying the quandary that I'm in,
    not distrusting you, either.
Let me have the spirit of the man you filled with wonder.
Let me remain by Mary
    as she assures me of her thoughtfulness
    and gently guides me to the time
    (when *you* decide the time to be)
    for witnessing whatever signs you choose
    to strengthen my belief in you
    and help me to be wonder-full.

Amen.

12

Mr. Downbut

Jesus took with him Peter and James and John and led them up a high mountain where they could be alone by themselves. There in their presence he was transfigured...

When they rejoined the disciples they saw a large crowd round them and some scribes arguing with them. The moment they saw him the whole crowd were struck with amazement and ran to greet him. "What are you arguing about with them?" he asked. A man answered him from the crowd, "Master, I have brought my son to you; there is a spirit of dumbness in him, and when it takes hold of him it throws him to the ground, and he foams at the mouth and grinds his teeth and goes rigid. And I asked your disciples to cast it out and they were unable to."

"You faithless generation," he said to them in reply. "How much longer must I be with you? How much longer must I put up with you? Bring him to me." They brought the boy to him and as soon as the spirit saw Jesus it threw the boy into convulsions, and he fell to the ground and lay writhing there, foaming at the mouth. Jesus asked the father, 'How long has this been happening to him?" "From childhood," he replied, "and it has often thrown him into the fire and into the water, in order to destroy him. But if you can do anything, have pity on us and help us." "If you can?" retorted Jesus. "Everything is possible for anyone who has faith." Immediately the father of the boy cried out, "I do have faith. Help the little faith I have!"

And Jesus...rebuked the unclean spirit, "Deaf and dumb spirit, I command you: come out of him and never enter him again." Then throwing the boy into violent convulsions it came out shouting, and the boy lay there so like a corpse that most of them said, "He is dead." But Jesus took him by the hand and helped him up, and he was able to stand.

Mark 9:2-28; Matthew 17:14-21
Luke 9:37-42

The first three Gospels tell the story of the man under study here. St. Mark gives us the most vivid account of him.

He has no name. He is presented as a man, a good man...but with a *but* at the end of all his goodness and with a *but* at the end of all his wrongness. He was a mixture, as we all are. He was a man of prayer, *but* not altogether so. He had faith, *but* he needed to be helped in his lack of faith. He sought help from God and God's disciples, *but* this didn't stop him from being angry, almost to the point of exasperation, when the healing did not happen. He was patient when cross-examined by our Lord, *but* he was impatient too over the apparently slow manner of Jesus' method of operating.

On the other hand, he was very, very discouraged, *but* not so discouraged that he quit trying or hoping or praying. He was down, but he was not out.

I'd like to give him the name "Mr. Downbut." This name begins with his negative characteristic, his depression and discouragement; it ends on the upbeat, that little bit of faith that he never let go of. God was able to do the rest.

The whole story has its ups and downs. Jesus and his three favorite disciples were just returning from the mountain where all four heard God declaring in a marvelous way that he loved Jesus, his Son, and was well-pleased with him. It was certainly a peak experience. Peter, James, and John wanted to remain, enjoying forever this sensible consolation. It did not happen. (It never does, in this life.)

After a brief experience of perfect bliss, our Lord said, "Let's go back down to the valley!" And back they went...and immediately the mood changed. There was bickering in the crowd, the sullen display of helplessness shown by the nine apostles left behind, and the hurt of disappointment on the face of Mr. Downbut: "Master, there is a spirit of dumbness in my son, and when it takes hold of him, it throws him to the ground and he foams at the mouth and grinds his teeth and goes rigid. And I asked your disciples to cast it out and they were unable to."

It must have been a sad scene all around. I don't wonder that the disciples were unable to cast out the demon. They had performed such miracles before (Mark 6:7-13; Matthew 10:1-14; Luke 9:1-6) but then they were cleanhearted and their heads were clear of jealousy. In this case, reading between the lines, it is easy to imagine they were not. They were envious and angry about the favoritism shown to Peter, James, and John. St. Luke mentions the rancour there was even at the Last Supper (22:24-27), so it is a good guess it existed here. Their hearts were divided between wanting to help the child and wishing they were someplace else. As a result, they could not work the healing. And the father of the possessed child had to be penalized for this strife within the community.

Whether or not this guess is correct, the man's hopes were shattered. His statement to Jesus was full of sadness. A sense of "being let down" was obvious. There might have been both anger and frustration in his voice.

At that very moment, as if to accentuate the helplessness of it all, the boy went into such a convulsion, as Mark depicts it, that only a Hollywood horror movie could do justice to.

Our Lord treated the whole scene so casually that it must have been exasperating to this man of little faith. It was as though Jesus were conversing with another doctor over a cup of coffee about a clinical case that happened months before. The boy was "writhing and foaming at the mouth" before his eyes, and Jesus asked the father to tell him the story of the sickness right from the start. The man tried to do so, but impatience soon got the better of him: "Look, here is my child in front of us, full of pain and agony! Master, *if* you can do anything, have pity on us and help us!"

Jesus replied, *"If* I can... Everything is possible for anyone who has faith." Jesus' words focused on the real problem. It is not a question of Christ's power to heal; it is a question of the man's faith... and the consistency of prayer that supports this faith, even when all things seem to go against it.

The man was equal to the challenge, once it was put to him in this way. He cried out, "I do have faith. Help the little faith I have!" (In older versions it was translated: "I do believe; help my disbelief!")

Then the healing took place; the prayers were finally answered.

The weak fingertip-hold of hope and faith was the means of Jesus' miracle. The man was down, *but* not completely. It was this little wedge of welcome to the power of Christ that made the whole thing happen.

There is a bit of "Mr. Downbut" in us all. Whether we are praying for ourselves or for someone else, there often seems to be a demoralizing slowness in the way Jesus answers our prayers. We get impatient very often, very impatient.

Within our own hearts, and in the hearts of others we pray for, there is an "offspring" that at times takes over with a kind of demoniacal control. We get hot with the fires of anger, possessed by bitterness and fierce resentment. Or we grow cold as ice — sullen and sulky — as though we were a catatonic corpse. We'd like to be rid of these moods. We pray for a healing of those we love, that they would be free of these moods as well.

And, so often, nothing happens... for such a long, long time. We try many remedies. We consult this doctor or that counselor; we attend this workshop or that retreat; we put our hopes in this favorite preacher, or healer, or in that author of a book on self-improvement. These are, doubtless, people of good will who helped others (as the nine Apostles had helped others up till then). But this time nothing works; the angry outbursts and the rigid behavior still remain.

And when we pray, Jesus seems so slow, so casual. He does not focus on what we want him to focus on, the trouble. Rather, he focuses on us, on our prayer and on our faith in him. He would have us understand the history, right from the beginning, of how the whole thing started, how long the anger or rigidity has been festering, how many other ways these unchecked emotions have held sway over our hearts. Above all, he wants us to increase our faith, to pray without giving up, to hope even when there seems to be no hope left.

It is a matter of control. When rancour and resentment control us (or others), and when humans can't seem to defuse these demons of possessiveness, then all must be placed in Christ's competence to rebuke our unclean spirits.

But we must want to be healed, unswervingly, without a whisper of fear to the contrary. We must not harbor the suspicion of "What's the use!" Frustration, whether wanted or not, will surface. The wonder about "What's the use!" will come from our feelings, even from fatigue. But fear, suspicion, and frustration must not come from

our mind and heart where decisions about life are ultimately made.
Faith — whatever shred of faith we still have — must be the teacher
controlling the rowdy class of these feelings.
    We must hold on to the little faith we still have. We must pray with
constant hope, like the man who happily found out that all things
possible did come true...after he blurted out his prayer, "I do
believe, Lord; help my disbelief."

Prayer of Mr. Downbut Within

Me, too, my Lord; me, too.
I have more confidence now,
        thanks to the Downbut person
        whose prayer you answered centuries ago.
I have more confidence in you
        and in me-with-you.

I am so often like that man
        in his impatience and exasperation.
I've prayed and prayed, so many times,
        for certain people;
I've tried to help them,
        as your disciples tried to heal that child,
        and nothing happened.
        I was no more successful than they were.
Also I've prayed and prayed
        about that "child" inside me
        — that brat within —
        who rages with resentment so bitterly
        that sometimes it possesses my whole person,
        and sometimes sulks
        and acts as if it, and I, were dead...and didn't care.

I've prayed and prayed.
And I've attended workshops,
        schools,
        and tried this remedy and that;
        with hope for healing, I put myself in a doctor's care
        and tried the methods of good guidancers
        who have helped others...but did not help me.

I am discouraged by the slow way healing happens.
I know you are with me through it all;
    but you are just *with* me —
    so casual, so nonchalant, it seems.

I want you to hurry up and do it;
you want me to understand the depths
    of what needs to be done
    — to let the roots be healed,
    not just my present and immediate discomfort.

I do have faith in you.
I will stand firm by you with me.
I'll pray, I promise, even when I feel like giving up
    and letting rage and rancour take over me all together.
I do have hope that everything is possible with you,
    once you are allowed to freely do what's yours to do.

I do have faith, Lord;
    only help the little faith I have.

Amen.

13

Minister Keep and Minister Going

The Lord appointed seventy-two others and sent them out ahead of him, in pairs, to all the towns and places he himself was to visit. He said to them, "The harvest is rich but the labourers are few, so ask the Lord of the harvest to send labourers to his harvest. Start off now, but remember, I am sending you out like lambs among wolves. Carry no purse, no haversack, no sandals. Salute no one on the road. Whatever house you go into, let your first words be, 'Peace to this house!' And if a man of peace lives there, your peace will go and rest on him; if not, it will come back to you. Stay in the same house, taking what food and drink they have to offer, for the labourer deserves his wages; do not move from house to house. Whenever you go into a town where they make you welcome, eat what is set before you. Cure those in it who are sick, and say, 'The kingdom of God is very near to you.'

"But when you enter a town and they do not make you welcome, go out into its streets and say, 'We wipe off the very dust of your town that clings to our feet, and leave it with you...'"

The seventy-two came back rejoicing. "Lord," they said, "even the devils submit to us when we use your name."

He said to them, "I watched Satan fall like lightning from heaven. Yes, I have given you power to tread underfoot serpents and scorpions and the whole strength of the enemy; nothing shall ever hurt you. Yet do not rejoice that the spirits submit to you; rejoice rather that your names are written in heaven."

It was then that, filled with joy by the Holy Spirit, he said, "I bless you, Father, Lord of heaven and earth, for hiding these things from the learned and the clever and revealing them to mere children. Yes, Father, for that is what it pleased you to do..."

Luke 10:1-21; 9:1-6
Mark 6:7-11; Matthew 10:1,5,9-14

*U*nlike the rest of the chapters in this book, the story of the Other Villagers has no scriptural basis whatsoever. We only have clues that it *might* have happened.

We do know that Jesus sent two groups of people on a mission. He "sent them out ahead of him, in pairs, to all the towns and places he himself was to visit." One group was his most select circle of Twelve (Luke 9; Matthew 10; Mark 6); the other group was the wider range of his followers. (Luke 10:1: "The Lord appointed seventy-two others and sent them out ahead of him...")

These disciples remain anonymous. One could make a case that Matthias and Barsabbas were members of this group (Acts 1:23), but we know little even about these.

The seventy-two were given the same instructions that the Apostles were given on a previous commission. The message itself seems to run in pairs, each set having a negative and then a positive statement. They could be paraphrased as follows:

1. Negative "Take nothing with you that would indicate distrust in God's providence. You are doing them a favor, caring for their spiritual needs; let them do you a favor, caring for your physical needs. Thus you will be simple and non-threatening in your deportment."

   Positive "Be single-minded in your message. Bless the people with God's blessing. Heal the sick. Encourage the discomfited. Release those who suffer from bondage to the devil. Prepare them for my visitation."

2. Negative "Do not act like gadflies, flitting from house to house. Stay where you first settled. Don't change accommodations according to your personal whim... or because another home might give you better meals."

Positive   "If you enter a town and they do not receive you or
listen to you, go forth from there and shake off the
dust from your feet as a witness against them. (Then
go to another village which will give you a more deserving welcome.)"

I have put the last parenthetical remark on our Lord's lips because
the context seems to indicate such a further instruction. Only a few
verses before the mission of the disciples, Jesus had done that very
thing: "He sent messengers ahead of him . . . to a Samaritan village to
make preparations . . . but the people would not receive him . . . Seeing this, James and John said, 'Lord, do you want us to call down
fire from heaven and burn them up?' But Jesus turned and rebuked
them and they went off to another village" (Luke 9:51-56).

After the model came the message. Our Lord first demonstrated
what was to be done. Then he told his followers to do the same.
Both the modeling and the message contain a warning against the
use of force, any kind of force.

James and John had a vindictive streak in them that belongs, it
seems, to a certain kind of do-gooder. There are people who really
want to help other people; no question about their good intentions.
But they want so much to help others that they get positively livid
when their chosen clients refuse their help. Then they want to
destroy those who so unceremoniously snubbed them.

Jesus rebuked James and John. In so doing, he warned all people
who offer help to others: "If they do not accept you, back off. Go
somewhere else and start again. Do not use force of any kind to
make people grow when they do not want to grow."

This lesson is important enough. Love is persuasive only when it
remains what it is. When love gets pushy, it ceases to be love.

But Jesus did more, here, than make his often-repeated rebuke to
the spirit of vengeance. It seems that he also gave instructions about
how to get away from a mood of discouragement — a particular kind
of discouragement common among those who minister to other
people's needs.

The situation is the same: suggested assistance is met with
ungracious rejection. Reaction to this branches off in two directions.
One way, the way of James and John, is to project blame on the
irresponsive others and let them know how wrong it was to have
refused our ministry.

The other way is to take all the blame upon ourselves, and wring
our hands with useless worry: "What did we do wrong? Why didn't

they even listen to us? We were only doing it for their own good."
This reaction surrenders any thought of going on to any other towns.
The desire to help just shrivels up with the disquieting evidence of
failure.

Both reactions are unproductive. Both show traces of wasteful
anger. In one, the anger is directed outward, on those who refuse
our help. In the other, the anger is directed inward — on ourselves,
for not succeeding in helping them. Our Lord warns his followers not
to be infected with either strain of this virus.

Since James and John were rebuked for having one side of this
characteristic, I have picked two of the unnamed disciples to demonstrate the other side of Christ's lesson.

They have no names, so permit me to call them Minister Keep and
Minister Going. "Minister" because that is what they were commissioned to do. One is named "Keep," the other "Going" to
preserve a balance between them.

They were good company for each other. Each provided a
strength where the other was weaker. I have visualized them going
off, without purse or satchel or sandals, but with hearts full of good
intentions and minds full of good instructions. They made it to the
first town. Jesus had predicted the reception some would get. These
two got stuck with the bad reception. Maybe they were hooted at.
Maybe they were just ignored. Whatever the details, they failed. No
matter what they tried, they could not communicate; they could not
get through.

It was time to switch over to "Plan B": "Go off to another village
and try again."

I imagine they did not simply move out right away, strolling down
the road as if nothing had happened. They were jolted out of all
composure, at least for awhile. Unrequited service is as hard to
manage as unrequited love. Both lover and minister feel jilted by
rebuff. It hurts.

They probably sat by the side of the road, bewildered, frustrated,
ready to condemn themselves, maybe even worried about what
Jesus might say when they turned up with a bad report card. Such a
mood, however, could not have remained with them for long. They
ended up with joyful news to share about their journey . . . and this
could not have resulted from the first town they came to.

They probably had a way of encouraging one another, brushing
themselves off, forgetting their failure, chalking it up to experience . . .
moving on.

If one had the characteristic of "keep" and the other of "going," it is easy to understand how they could be mutually supportive. The first functioned as an introvert; the other supplied enough extrovertive sensitivity for both of them.

And introvert keeps. He does not get too excited when others heartily accept him; he does not get too disheartened when others dismiss him. He knows his value. He does not depend on outside responses. Jesus loved him and gave him authority to preach and the power to heal people in the name of God. Such love and power was still his, whether others availed themselves of it or not. "That's all right," he might have said to his associate, "we still have our instructions and we still have the ability to follow them. Those people didn't take away anything of ourselves. We aren't incapacitated by this failure. We have kept all the essentials."

This is the kind of assurance the extrovert would need in such a situation. Left all to himself, Mr. Going would have been devastated. He would have tended to rely overmuch on impressions that came from outside himself. If the townsfolk liked him, he was likeable; if they appreciated the good he did for them, he was worthwhile. If they disdained his person and rejected his deeds, he believed himself to be no good and he judged his kindness to be of no worth.

Minister Keep would have been there to remind him that his goodness continued to be with him. It was God who graced him, Jesus who commissioned him. No unfavorable response could eradicate these inward realities.

Then the extrovert would have helped the introvert. Once confidence was re-established, hope could be restored. Minister Keep, if left to himself, could have stayed right there until it was time to go home. He would have remained composed, self-contained, perhaps idly marveling at the stupidity of some people, perhaps mildly judging the bad manners of the people in the town just left.

It would have been his friend who got them on the road again. One quality of the extrovert is a lively sensitivity to others. Minister Going would have a way of finishing up one episode and preparing for the next. "Let's go, friend," he might have said; "leave those people to somebody else. Maybe the time's not ripe yet. Maybe other disciples will reach them later on. God will see to it, somehow.

"Meanwhile, we have work to do. There's a village just three miles north of here. I'm sure they have as many needs as these people. They might be the very ones that we are meant to serve."

And so they did. Their second try was quite successful. I assume this to be so. My basis is St. Luke's conclusion: "The seventy-two came back rejoicing. 'Lord,' they said, 'even the devils submit to us when we use your name.'" (10:17). That is an all-inclusive report. No set of disciples drew a blank. I'm only guessing that *everything* didn't go smoothly for *all* of them. That's not the normal way things happen. Besides, why would Jesus tell them what to do in case of rejection if there were no possibility of rejection? Putting together both Christ's instruction and the odds against total acceptance of any proposal, no matter how good, I presume that at least one pair met with at least one clinker.

No matter. Jesus said to all of them: "Rejoice, most of all, in the fact that your names are written in the book of life" (Luke 10:20). God loved them all — even the half-successful — because they tried. God loved them on a first-name basis because they loved Jesus and cared enough to want to do good works in Jesus' name.

There was a wonderful celebration when everybody returned. As St. Luke remembers it, the mood was jubilant, like that displayed in the locker room by the world series winners. It is the only time in the Gospels where Jesus is said to have rejoiced. The phrase was exuberant — our Lord was *"filled* with joy." (The Greek word that the Evangelist used indicates "dancing up and down with exhilaration;" it certainly indicates much more than a carefully-placed smile on the lips.) No doubt Jesus was joyful often. But the only time that care was taken to mention it was at the happy reunion of his seventy-two missionaries.

I wonder about other celebrations that were going on at the same time. There had to be at least thirty-six villages which benefitted from this spiritual and physical redevelopment program. The sick were healed; the grief-stricken were given hope; the compulsively addicted and the neurotic were freed from the satanic power that bound them. Every town had its story to tell; every home had its reason to be joyful.

I like to think about the good news the "other village" spread — the second one visited by Minister Keep and Minister Going. Their story would be similar to all the other towns that received help and used the opportunity to reject sin, rejuvenate faith, restore dignity in themselves, and reclaim their hope in a saving God.

This village would have one thing further to add. Their story would also include gratitude for what the two disciples did not do: "Thanks be to God, forever! We were healed of our woes and instructed in the faith of Christ. It could so easily have turned out otherwise. We did not head the list of towns to be covered. When the Lord's disciples met with rejection at their first try, they might have just stayed there, sulking by the side of the road. They could have sulked. We would not blame them if they did. It's only natural to brood over failure. It's normal for people to give up on everybody after they've been hit with a bitter disappointment.

"We didn't really expect them to forget their wounds so quickly. We marvel at the way they shook off the dust of their depression and tried again. They didn't stop loving just because some people refused to love them back.

"We remember how shy they were when they first arrived in town. They imagined that we would give them the same bad treatment. But we didn't. We welcomed them warmly. There was every reason to do so. We needed what they had to give; and they gave it. Now all the people in our village are healed, hopeful, and happy once again. Why shouldn't we be filled with joy? We will never forget our debt of gratitude for those two disciples who cared about our needs more than they cared about their own frustrations."

There may be some doubt that the story of the "Other Villagers" was ever told in just this way. But there is no doubt that the challenge ascribed to the two unnamed disciples is a challenge every individual faces, many times more than once.

We have all failed one way or another . . . somebody . . . sometime . . . somehow. It's not so much that others have let us down, although crushed expectations are certainly a part of the hurt. What goes on inside is more a feeling that we have let them down, accompanied by an even worse feeling that we have let ourselves down. The feelings produce a mood like a dense fog settling over everything. The mood keeps interrogating itself with such aimless questions as "Where did I go wrong?" "How did I do wrong?" "What's the matter with me?" It then proceeds to make global statements about uselessness in general and other self-deprecating remarks.

We know the heaviness of such an experience. Everyone has suffered from it. Each person has a different story to tell.

A family wants to help an addict or alcoholic, and the person does not want to change. Parents try to steer one of their children toward some other road, any road but the pernicious one he or she is on, and the youngster will not listen. Friend will try to rescue friend from a self-destructive course of moping around the house, and the friend prefers the lassitude of sadness to any offers of encouragement. A worker tries to talk sense to the boss about improving things and she might as well talk to the wall. A concerned person tries to ease the tension in the rectory, convent, hospital, social organization, but the person causing the tension refuses to be moved.

Then comes the envelope of frustration, fomenting the reaction of anger. Sometimes anger is hurled outward — nag the alcoholic, kick the kid out of the house, start a smear campaign against the friend who won't listen to reason, lead a mutiny against the boss, or rail against those people who cause tension in the group — all different versions of the alternative brought up by James and John: "Bring out firepower and destroy those who refuse to accept help!" This alternative, of course, was sternly rebuked by Jesus.

There is another way to express our anger. This is the more popular alternative. It is still anger, but the anger now is turned in upon ourselves. We don't give others a piece of our mind. We let them steal from us a piece of our own heart. A large piece, usually. We get angry at ourselves. We assess ourselves a failure, a much greater failure than the one relationship would warrant. We "sit by the side of the road" and give up on everything.

A family member can forget the others in the family and a whole circle of friends because one alcoholic looms so large that everybody else fades out of mind. Parents can become so upset over the one son who went wrong that they lose all concern over their other children. These have as much right to their parents as the problem child; but they cannot claim this right because their parents have filled themselves with useless self-pity and soured the home with their joyless anxiety. A woman faced with a failure at work can let the forty hours of her week take over the rest of the week . . . and family and friends, and even God, are neglected because of all the negative attention she gives to her problems at work.

Examples are endless. Teachers consider themselves no good if they cannot reach five — or even one! — of their class of thirty students. They neglect the twenty-five they could be reaching because all life has gone out of them since their rejection by the five. Priests, workers for social justice, counselors, people in all aspects of the helping professions, frequently suffer from the temptation to quit because failure has made them frustrated, then angry at themselves.

These situations are always serious. They challenge our own self-worth; they make us wonder whether our goodness is any good at all. Because they are so serious — they are turning points in our lives — we need to cultivate the spirit displayed by Minister Keep and Minister Going.

One was an introvert; one an extrovert. In reality, though, all people are made up of a combination of the two. Some have more of one, some more of the other; but we all have both characteristics within ourselves. To some degree we all act out of principles formed from within, *and* we are sensitive to other people, caring about their response to us and forming judgments of ourselves based on their responses.

Let the introvert side of us (the "Minister Keep" within) remember that our worth does not depend on any particular success or failure. Our worth comes from what God has given us. Rejection cannot take it away from us, as though we were a television show that had to slink out of sight as soon as it got a bad Nielsen rating. Let the introvert side of us keep balance.

Then let the extrovert side (the "Minister Going" within) get us going again. There are those "other children" in our family... those "other friends" we can reach... those "other twenty-five students" who need our help... those "other hours" in the week when we aren't working... those "other villagers" who wait for us to shake the dust off our failures and go to them.

The "other villagers" of our lives have a story they want to tell. It's all about help, and healing, and hope, and good things received from God. But they cannot begin to tell their story unless we start it off for them. Then they can be filled with joy.

We too can be joyful, thanks to them, as we return to Jesus and tell him all that happened, the pluses and the minuses. We won't have to worry; we tried. Jesus will "thrill for joy" no less than he did the first time, and we will be reminded that we are entered — on a first-name basis — in God's book of everlasting life.

Prayer of Ministers Keep and Going Within

Jesus, my Lord,
    defend me from my moodiness
    when I have failed to help
    someone I wanted to
    someone I thought you, somehow, sent to me.
The times of my successes please me hugely.
Then my morale is high
    — as high as the disciples' was
    when they returned with their fine reports.

But when I get a snub of any kind,
    a bark to back off,
    or a wordlessly-expressed dismissal of my presence,
    then I'm demoralized.
The best in me seems to get all slumped over
    and I just want to quit.
It's not so much that I get mad at my refusers
    (though that's there too) . . .
It's more disappointment with myself:
    a bad taste in my mouth
    that chews on words like
    worthless, what's the use, why bother anymore.

Help me to shake off sadness.
Tell me what you told your first disciples:
    to shake the dust of their refusal back on them
    — it's their responsibility, their free will to refuse.
You will judge them, not I.
And you will, doubtless, send them other ministers
    who will have the right approach,
    the right occasion
    to help them in the ways I couldn't.
Meanwhile, there are other towns ahead,
    — more than I could ever hope to handle.
There will be many others
    who will receive me graciously
    and give me love and friendship,
    offering opportunities to help them
    and to be helped by them.

Keep me aware of all the "keep" you've given me:
Your grace and love, your Spirit and instructions
    cannot be forfeited by anyone's rejection.
And keep me going,
    undaunted by discouragement;
    so that, at the end of all the life
    and all the journeys that you give me,
    I, too, can hear the stories of my "other villagers"
    ...and I, too, can be filled with joy.

Amen.

14
Lady Devirtnoc

One of the Pharisees invited [the Lord] to a meal. When he arrived at the Pharisee's house and took his place at table, a woman came in, who had a bad name in the town. She had heard he was dining with the Pharisee and had brought with her an alabaster jar of ointment. She waited behind him at his feet, weeping, and her tears fell on his feet, and she wiped them away with her hair; then she covered his feet with kisses and anointed them with the ointment.

When the Pharisee who had invited him saw this, he said to himself, "If this man were a prophet, he would know who this woman is that is touching him and what a bad name she has."

Then Jesus took him up and said, "Simon, I have something to say to you." "Speak, Master" was the reply. "There was once a creditor who had two men in his debt; one owed him five hundred denarii, the other fifty. They were unable to pay, so he pardoned them both. Which of them will love him more?" "The one who was pardoned more, I suppose," answer Simon. Jesus said, "You are right."

Then he turned to the woman. "Simon," he said, "you see this woman? I came into your house, and you poured no water over my feet, but she has poured out her tears over my feet and wiped them away with her hair. You gave me no kiss, but she has been covering my feet with kisses ever since I came in. You did not anoint my head with oil, but she has anointed my feet with ointment. For this reason I tell you that her sins, her many sins, must have been forgiven her, or she would not have shown such great love. It is the man who is forgiven little who shows little love." Then he said to her, "Your sins are forgiven."

115

Those who were with him at table began to say to themselves, "Who is this man, that he can forgive sins?" But he said to the woman, "Your faith has saved you; go in peace."

Luke 7:36-50

I would like to call her Lady because Simon the Pharisee thought of her as anything but a lady. Even though she has no name in the Gospel of St. Luke, I've given her the title of nobility to dramatize Christian respect for her in contrast to the Pharisee's disdain.

She has a last name: "Devirtnoc." This, too, is a designation-by-contrast. Devirtnoc is the word *contrived* spelled backward. A contriver is a schemer, an artful planner of things, a devisor ahead of time, a manipulator of environment and people. The woman called "she who had a bad name in town" — or even more simply, "the sinner" — was just the opposite. Far from being a contriver, she was spontaneous to the point of effusiveness.

It is good to have a name that emphasizes the difference between her and the Pharisees. This seems to be the whole point our Lord is making... St. Luke, too.

We cannot just call her "sinner." There is no contrast made by that word. All people are sinners; all are in need of God's grace and forgiveness. Might as well call someone "a person who breathes," "a woman who needs to eat," "a man who must sleep," "a mortal who has to die." Considering such matters, we are all in it together. Likewise, we are all sinners.

Simon the Pharisee did not think so. Doubtless, he would not argue against those other equalities, such as the need for air and food and sleep and the fact of death. But it would certainly surprise him to be likened to Lady Devirtnoc regarding the fact of sinfulness and the need of God's mercy.

He thought he was pretty good. Certainly, he considered himself very good compared to her who was "very bad." He knew the rules of right conduct and he kept them. He had studied the Law and had sought the truth. Even on the present occasion, he was displaying the fact that he searched for wisdom over and beyond the call of duty. Had he not (patronizingly?) invited the itinerant preacher, Jesus of Nazareth, to dine in his house? With hospitable humility, he had prepared himself to learn something from the Galilean. He was at least open enough to honor Jesus with the title "Master," or Teacher.

But that seemed to be as far as he would go. The normal gestures of respect were left undone, unsaid. The whole scene suggests what would happen today if a renowned professor from a prestigious university were to invite a self-made but uneducated person to dinner. The whole meeting would be masterminded by the professor. He would be acutely aware of his overall superiority, but the young prophet might possibly have fresh insights or new ways of expressing what the Academy already knew so well. There would be a certain amount of deference to the newcomer; but there would not be the normal protocol of good manners, for where was the equality between a respected man-of-letters and a relatively untutored preacher-to-the-public?

It seems to have been something like this. Jesus complains about the snub he received: no welcoming kiss; no water to bathe his sandaled feet, which was as ordinary a gesture of welcome, at that time, as taking a guest's coat and hanging it up; no anointing the head with oil, which would be as commonplace as offering a glass of wine or cup of tea today.

The whole scene was characterized by a certain stiffness. Simon thought the honor went from him to Jesus, not the other way around. Simon was prepared to pick the brains of this popular hero. Perhaps he contrived to use that evening's conversation in an address to the next convocation of Pharisees, something like "New Religious Developments in the World Today." Whatever it was, with all his snobbery and snubbery, he was not prepared for the developments that actually occurred.

The first shock was the appearance of the uninvited guest. She didn't look like a lady; she didn't act like one, either. She supplied, lavishly and lovingly, all the signs of welcome that Simon had neglected. She wept and her tears fell on Jesus' feet and she wiped them away with her hair; then she covered his feet with kisses and anointed them with oil.

She was called a sinner. It does not mention what kind of sin made her notorious. Most likely, it was prostitution. In Matthew's Gospel (21:31), Jesus warns the Pharisees that "tax-collectors and prostitutes are making their way into the kingdom of God before you." This woman was most probably one of those Jesus spoke of.

Assuming this to be so, she did the most natural things she could think of. She was, one might say, a pleaser by trade. Perhaps she had taken note of what was left undone by Simon the host. Perhaps not. It really doesn't matter. Something within her was stirred. Hope surged through all her being. She somehow felt new life . . . and it was coming, somehow, from Jesus. She could change her ways, be forgiven of wrongdoing. She could hold her head up in public; she could be a lady at last.

She brought the perfume with her. This was the only part of her behavior that was in any way planned. Maybe even this was artless: a spur-of-the-moment gathering of precious ointment as she rushed to the house where Jesus was. The rest of her actions were certainly unplanned. The weeping was not just a few tears. It was a river of compunction, a compulsive flushing accompanied by great relief. The drying with the hair and the kissing of our Lord's feet — these too were most spontaneous. They were as uncontrived as anything can be. She gave Jesus the most precious things she had, tears, hair, lips, ointment. The last three had been the "tools of her trade." The tears were her waters of baptism into new life. It was as if she intuitively knew the right ritual, the right way to forswear her past and dedicate herself to the new life that was ushered in that night. She would be both a disciple of Jesus Christ and his hospitable host who, unlike the Pharisee, welcomed the Master with gracious signs of care and accommodation.

Our Lord's response to her was indirect. St. Luke notes that Jesus turned his attention to Simon. Jesus knew what the man was thinking and decided to comment on his prejudice. He did so by telling a story about two debtors who owed unequal amounts to a creditor. Jesus got Simon to admit that the man who had been released from the larger debt would have more reason to be thankful than the one released from the lesser one. The story pointed out the contrast between Simon's cold rudeness and the warm solicitation ministered by the disreputable woman.

This story implies that forgiveness of the woman came first. The woman somehow experienced *her* version of "debts released;" from the sense of mercy came her gratitude; from gratitude came relief; from relief came release of tears . . . and then came all those other acts that showed how much she loved. The Jerusalem Bible translation brings this out: "Her sins, her many sins, *must have been* forgiven her, or she would not have shown such great love."

Other translations imply that the woman's love came first. "Her many sins are forgiven *because* she has loved much." This wording suggests that she was the one who took the initiative; Christ's mercy followed her love.

It may be that it did happen this way — out of love for Jesus, she made him feel welcome; because of this, our Lord rewarded her with his gifts of pardon and peace. More likely, it was the other way around — by some sort of grace-filled hunch, she sensed the fact that her many sins were absolved; she then responded in the ways that showed much love.

Whichever moving force triggered the other, we do know that both mercy and love were eminently alive in her. We also know that neither mercy nor love could have begun to work unless she sensed her need.

Unlike Simon the Pharisee, she knew she was a sinner; she was aware that her life was worth little without God's help. Lady Devirtnoc was not a contriver. She was impulsively warm in her welcome and spontaneously right in her gestures of gratitude. She threw her needs, and then her tears, at Jesus' feet. Our Lord simply celebrated out loud what had already happened within her heart; she was saved by faith and generous love and allowed to go in peace.

There is a bit of both Simon the Pharisee and Lady Devirtnoc in us all. Our work — indeed, our fundamental work — is to weaken the one and strengthen the other.

The attitude represented by Simon is the tendency of the contriver and the comparer, the spirit that says "I am better than others" and "I am not in need." The "I am better" attitude fosters the other one. Both are really the same perversity.

Simon first congratulated himself that he was better than the woman of ill-repute. He was honoring Jesus by simply inviting him to supper. He was also dishonored by having a notorious woman break into the party. There seems to be grades of esteem. Simon: most honorable; Jesus: less honorable; the woman: dishonorable. From such an advantage of respectability, how could he even dream that he might be just as needy as the person he disdained?

So it is with all who consistently act out of the "Simon Syndrome." If I feel I am smarter or better or more adroit or more considerate than others, I place myself in a mental fix that doesn't owe anybody anything...including God. "Why should I be so grateful for Christ's grace that is offered to me for the forgiveness of my sins? What sins? It's the other people Jesus must have come for. They are the ones that need shaping up!"

Out of this mental fix evolves the contriving spirit. Contrivers do not ask for things straightforwardly. Honest admission implies neediness. Contrivers obtain things by trickery, indirection, stratagems. They will act like Simon — politely inviting Jesus to dine, hoping to get something out of him, but refusing any show of affection that might suggest a suitor asking for real help.

Not many of us act *consistently* this way. We do it sometimes, though. It must be recognized for the wrong it is and be checked.

We also act as Lady Devirtnoc acted. We certainly did so when we were children. Children live in the state of need. Except for their fantasies and fairy tales, nothing tells them anything different; they owe large debts all over the place. They are on the receiver's end of learning, food, clothes, toys, medical care, affirmation, security... just about everything. It is easy for them to respond in their own way as graciously as Lady Devirtnoc did.

This is religion in its most fundamental sense — grateful love springing from a gift received; a gift is appreciated because a need is acknowledged.

Certain human events bring out this joyful expression in adults as well. Such events are usually dramatic: a friend's bankroll covering some financial disaster, a firefighter or life guard saving one from death, a hero averting an epidemic or war.

Ordinary assistance, however, is harder to respond to. It's not that we aren't grateful; we usually save up cumulative goodness done to us and show our gratitude on certain marked occasions. That's what birthdays and anniversaries and other festivals are for. They are very important. They help us reduce our tendency to take people for granted. This tendency would pave the way for the contriver spirit.

Adults have real difficulty in showing gratitude in the area of religion. God's gifts are devalued because our needs are not acknowledged or admitted to ourselves. Our sins are not acknowledged as honestly as the repentant prostitute acknowledged hers. But all of us are sinners; all of us have needs. If Jesus died and rose for all, died and rose for the forgiveness of sins, then every one of us is classified with the man in the story whose large debt was cancelled... not the one who owed only a little bit.

The woman in the Gospel can help us develop the most basic aspects of religion: humility and the sense of receivership. We are mortals, afraid of dying, with only hope in Christ's resurrection to save us from the dread of nothingness. We are corrupters of ourselves, manipulators of others, escape-artists of life's demands — that is, we are sinners. It is not in our power to heal ourselves into wholeness or put ourselves on the path to peace. This is Christ's work. Only he can do it; and he will do it just as he promised . . . as long as we realize how much we need it.

All else, celebrated so charmingly by Lady Devirtnoc, follows from this fundamental attitude. Jesus responds to us with mercy. We experience a marvelous sensation of serenity. Guilt is released and the desire for goodness is renewed. Then, filled as we are with God's favor, we show our love for others as sensitively as the woman showed her love for our Lord. We begin to give great love because we have been loved much, very much.

Prayer of Lady Devirtnoc Within

Jesus, my Lord,
    protect me from my contrivances.
Put me at a distance
    from complacency about all my belongings
    and especially from that claim of belonging to myself.
Don't let me exploit anyone in my search
    for love or truth.
    Don't let me think I'm better than my fellow-sinners.
I am a sinner, too:
I fear death,
    have a dread of loneliness,
    haven't all the answers.

Give me the spirit of that woman
    whose sins you pardoned centuries ago.
I need her spirit now.
I need to know my own needs better
    — my great neediness —
    so that I can return to your mercy
    and then respond with much love back
    in ways befitting all my debts forgiven.

Don't let me throw away the gifts I have
    because I sometimes sinned misusing them.
The woman in the Gospel misused her gifts.
She cared for others, sensitive to please;
    but she had sullied these good qualities
    and traded graciousness for gain.

You did not tell her not to care.
You praised her for her pleasing ways with you,
    but this was after you forgave her,
    when she no longer used her gifts contrivingly.

So let me get my good gifts back
    and use them with impulsive warmth,
    as she did.
Let me be spontaneous with goodness
    simply because it's good to do so.
It's the best way I can go in peace,
    the best way I can show you my great love.

Amen.

15

Captain Workalogic

When Jesus had come to the end of all he wanted the people to hear, he went into Capernaum. A centurion there had a servant, a favorite of his, who was sick and near death. Having heard about Jesus he sent some Jewish elders to him to ask him to come and heal his servant. When they came to Jesus they pleaded earnestly with him. "He deserves this of you," they said, "because he is friendly towards our people; in fact, he is the one who built the synagogue."

So Jesus went with them, and was not very far from the house when the centurion sent word to him by some friends: "Sir," he said, "do not put yourself to trouble; because I am not worthy to have you under my roof; and for this same reason I did not presume to come to you myself; but give the word and let my servant be cured. For I am under authority myself, and have soldiers under me; and I say to one man: Go, and he goes; to another: Come here, and he comes; to my servant: Do this, and he does it."

When Jesus heard these words, he was astonished at him and, turning round, said to the crowd following him, "I tell you, not even in Israel have I found faith like this."

And when the messengers got back to the house they found the servant in perfect health.

Luke 7:1-10; Matthew 8:5-13

*T*he Evangelists Luke and Matthew call him simply "a Centurion."
The Jews called him benefactor: "He loves us well; he built our synagogue." Jesus called him a person whose faith surpassed anyone
else's in all Israel. I would like to call him "Captain Workalogic."

"Captain" is easily understood. It is the rank in today's army for a
commander of a company of soldiers. In the Roman Legion a
company consisted of 100 men; the head of this "century" was a
centurion.

The last name "Workalogic" is a bit more belabored. It is not, of
course, an actual name; rather, it signifies the man's most admirable
characteristic. He was a worker, not in the sense of a "workaholic;"
just the opposite. Work did not give him compulsiveness, leading to
a sick mind; it gave him logic, leading to a sound theology.

He took pride in his duties; he was a task-oriented person. He did
not say that Jesus ought to do him a favor because he was a
generous person. His provision of money and labor for the building
of the synagogue was something he had done on his own.

The soldier emphasized what he did on the job. He knew how to
obey orders from his higher-ups. He was trustworthy, and prided
himself on this. Also and more to the point, he knew how to give
orders. He had earned the respect of the men under him. They had
confidence in his ability to lead. There were no questions asked, no
insubordination. The captain gave an order and the order was
obeyed. The chain of command ran smoothly because he handled
authority well.

This was the "base of operations" from which faith went to work
upon his logic. Faith was a gift that came to him, unearned. Faith
told him Jesus was a man of God, a prophet, a lover of everyone, a
healer of all forms of sickness. Jesus could command evil to leave a
person's body. All the elements of nature, all the maladies that infect
a human, and all the devils of discouragement that possess a human
— everything on this earth was subject to Christ's control. The ills of
life were subject to Jesus as enlisted men were subject to their company commander. This much the centurion knew by faith.

Then came the logic. "If such be the case," the Captain must have
mused as he waited for our Lord's approach, "then only the word of
commands needs to be said. Jesus is always at his best in these matters. Then he must be as I am at my best...when I am doing my job
right. If I say 'Do it,' the job is done. Therefore, all he needs to say is
'Do it.' This makes sense to me. He need come no closer. I will send
my friends to him and tell him: 'Lord, I am not worthy to have you
under my roof. You need only give the word and my servant will be

cured.'"

Surely, the soldier knew about Jesus before this event. Perhaps he knew the Master's teaching too. Perhaps he had listened to Jesus talking about the right use of logic in the parable of "Bread, not Stones." He must have known about the parable, at least by hearsay.

Our Lord based his teaching on ordinary interchange. He asked us to think about our commonplace, day-in and day-out relationships. Then, using logic, he linked revelation about God to what we already know about ourselves.

The revelation was that God is a loving Father, always responsive to our needs. The way Jesus explained this revelation was by telling us to think about our own experiences, when we are at our best, responding sensitively to the needs of other people. We are to build our image of God from this raw material. Jesus put it this way: "If someone asks you for bread (that is, for kindness, care, concern, love) you would not give a stone instead . . . If you, then, know how to give what is good, how much more will your Father in heaven give good things to those who ask him."

The phrase "how much *more*" is the link between our ordinary love for others and God's magnificent love for us. God is like us when we are good to others . . . only he is better; he is "much more."

The Centurion understood this teaching. He seemed to understand it better than anyone in Israel. He put a new twist on it; he added a new dimension. The man not only sensed God's loving care for him and his servant; he also had a sense for the way God was able to demonstrate this care. Jesus did not have to rely on intermediaries. He did not have to be actually present in the place of healing, as though he were held down by time and space, or had to "psyche up" the audience before anything could happen. All he had to do was say "Do it!" and it would be done.

This was the logic of the man's faith. It was the "Bread, not Stones" parable applied in a practical way. The Centurion understood that love was not just a nice abstraction, a general attitude. It was an accomplishing thing — it was *deeds,* issued by a commander with all the serene assurance that the Centurion himself had when he was giving military orders to soldiers in the field.

No wonder Jesus gave the man such superlative praise: "Even in Israel I have not found faith like this." Faith is belief in *someone.* It is other-directed. The emphasis is on what God can do, and perhaps wills to do. Faith does not concentrate on what *I* want done. Others in Israel made more of their own needs than of Christ's capabilities: "I'm a leper," they pleaded . . . "I've a daughter sick at home" . . . "I'm

tired of coming to this well to draw water"... "My child is possessed"
... "Do something!"

Jesus gladly did it. He answered all their prayers. But done this way, the emphasis is likely to remain subjective. There is gratitude to God, of course. But most of the energy is spent reflecting on the favor received than on the God who gave it. Jesus had trouble establishing a continuity of relationship. Subjectivism made things sporadic. It was hard to nourish any kind of faith-development when people felt need, asked help, received healing, praised God... and then went on their way.

Captain Workalogic placed the possibilities for healing in a better perspective. He did not deny the need — the servant he loved was sick. But the focus of his prayer, on our Lord's ability to do the work, had more staying power. Grace could lead to more grace because faith continued to be directed toward Jesus, who was the base of operations.

Surely, the soldier refused to stoop to the bartering system of the Scribes and Pharisees. Theirs was a theology our Lord was always in conflict with. They thought: "We have done this and that and the other things... and paid our Temple tax... and scrupulously avoided things unclean. Therefore, God has to reward us in ways we think are due." According to this thinking (it is only suggested by Luke) the Pharisees would have the Centurion say something like this: "Look, Jesus, I've done a lot of good for your people. It was quite a drain on my wallet to build such a lovely synagogue in Capernaum. I didn't mind. I'm a big-hearted guy. All I ask in return is to heal my favorite servant who is sick and near death. After all I've done, I think I've got it coming to me!"

The man said nothing of the kind. This would be a "cheap shot," a kind of intimidation of divinity. He refused to mention any deeds that might label him benefactor or good person; he concentrated on his unworthiness. In relationship to God's gifts of life, hope, and healing, what is so persuasive about donating a synagogue or a hospital or putting ten dollars in the collection basket? The man was God-directed, task-oriented and self-submissive. He was on the receiving end of grace. He knew Jesus could work the miracle; it would be done if it were the right time to do it.

The miracle was done. Everything was in good order. We don't know what happened afterward. The man is not mentioned again. Chances are, he steadily grew in grace. For twenty centuries, the Catholic Church has grown from the impetus of his brief statement. "Lord," we pray just before receiving the Body of Christ, "I am not

worthy to receive you, but only say the word and I shall be healed."
Then we receive our Lord. This is a gift, not something we have
earned. Although we admit our need of healing, our prayer is not so
much focused on ourselves as it is on Christ's power to nourish and
sustain us. Attention is centered on the Person who is about to give
us Bread, not stones.

When we are at our best, our faith is the same faith Captain Workalogic expressed; our words are even the same as his. Please God,
we will be blessed with the same praise he received: "I tell you, I have
not found faith like this."

As mentioned earlier, the name Workalogic was chosen because
of its contrast to workaholic. A workaholic suffers from compulsive
behavior...like all the other "aholics." Such a person is caught up in
his or her job, swallowed by it. It compensates for every other relationship and responsibility. It is a means of escape and often causes
as much suffering as an alcoholic may bring to family and friends.

So much has been written lately about the pitfalls of workaholism
that there is a danger of going to the other extreme. We can begin to
devalue the whole idea of work. We can shrug off a large section of
our lives with statements like: "Get the job done, punch the time
clock, leave factory or office...and then move into the business of
really living!"

Certainly, we are more than who we are at our job. Our value is
greater than what our paycheck discloses. Our interests and relationships are broader than our careers. Even so, our work is (or could be)
very important, not only in itself and in its necessary function of
giving us the means for survival, but also in the way it can help us
understand God better.

As a rule, people are at their best when they are on the job. Not
always, but often. We can work together to get a spacecraft on the
moon or to host the Olympics better than we can settle neighborhood
difficulties or a family squabble. If the job does not give satisfaction,
there is usually a hobby that will serve this purpose. Something —
even if it's a common and undistinguished accomplishment such as
teaching Boy Scouts how to tie knots — something in every person's
life can produce that feeling of efficiency that Captain Workalogic
displayed so admirably.

It would be a good idea to nourish our faith a la Centurion. To
think of God only in relation to our weakness can keep our prayers

all too subjective and focused only on ourselves. In subjective prayer, God is put into a bind — either he *has to* answer our petitions, or if he doesn't, he is just as weak as we are. Then down the drain goes faith, and prayer with it. "What's the sense of asking God for help or healing?" we will say. "He is just as powerless, as uncaring, as we are ...only worse!"

Jesus taught us that God is just as caring as we are, when we are at our best, only he is *better*. That is the message of the "Bread, not Stones" parable. Jesus also implied — by his heart-glad response to the soldier — that God is as powerful as we are when we are working at our best and fully in control. Of course, God is more powerful — the work of his hands is all creation and the new creation of Christ's saving purposes. But we can understand God's ability to work for our well-being when we think of him from the logic of our own well-done jobs.

There is a Captain Workalogic in us all. Like him, we can keep our faith from sputtering as long as we remember that God is so good with his power and so powerful in his goodness that he can work miracles from any distance. He only has to say the word and we shall be made whole.

Prayer of Captain Workalogic Within

Jesus, my Lord,
    help me to be better on the job.
Give me more calm,
        freed from the hectic pace,
        the frenzied hassles of demandingness,
        the worry about too much going on ...

Let me find ways to like myself for what I do.
Help me forgive those people I don't like:
        the unjust,
        the slipshod,
        the irritating characters at work.
Don't let this cranky minority
        destroy my honest pride in my achievements.
And don't let my own bad days, or imperfections,
        frustrate me to the point
        of thinking I'm not any good at all.

Let me be like that Centurion you praised.
He must have had bad days, too;
   and chafed under thoughtless orders from his superiors.
He must have been irritated, at times,
   by the heedlessness of some subordinates.
But, for the most part, he was who he was — good;
   and he did what he did — well;
   and he took pride in both.

Give me the practical wisdom to do the same —
   one day at a time.
Then let me pray:
"Lord, I am not worthy that you should come to me;
   but I remember how I do my tasks:
   I know how to take orders
   and I know how to give them;
   I can follow through and see that things get done.

"This is my world of work.
My faith in you builds on this world of mine.
I know you are like me at my best —
   only you are better in your goodness;
   greater in your authority.

"I wait upon your word
   which waits upon your will.
I am not worthy you should come to me;
   but all you need to do is say your word
   and I will be nourished, sustained in faith, and healed."

Amen.

16
Master Christmas

When Jesus returned to Capernaum some time later, word went round that he was back; and so many people collected that there was no room left, even in front of the door. He was preaching the word to them when some people came bringing him a paralytic carried by four men, but as the crowd made it impossible to get the man to him, they stripped the roof over the place where Jesus was; and when they had made an opening, they lowered the stretcher on which the paralytic lay. Seeing their faith, Jesus said to the paralytic, "My child, your sins are forgiven."

Now some Scribes were sitting there, and they thought to themselves, "How can this man talk like that? He is blaspheming. Who can forgive sins but God?"

Jesus, inwardly aware that this was what they were thinking, said to them, "Why do you have these thoughts in your hearts? Which of these is easier to say to the paralytic, 'Your sins are forgiven' or to say, 'Get up, pick up your stretcher and walk'? But to prove to you that the Son of Man has authority on earth to forgive sins" — he said to the paralytic — "I order you: get up, pick up your stretcher, and go home."

And the man got up, picked up his stretcher at once and walked out in front of everyone, so that they were all astounded and praised God saying, "We have never seen anything like this."

Mark 2:1-12; Luke 5:17-26
Matthew 9:1-8

131

The story of the paralytic lying on the stretcher is a very important one. All three Gospels suggest that it took place early in our Lord's ministry. It seems to be a "hinge event." It brought on the first serious clash with the Scribes and Pharisees.

But while all three Gospels devote a comparatively large amount of space to developing the story, very little is known about the man himself. We not only don't know his name; we don't know much about his personality, either. To understand this unnamed individual, we have to do a lot of guessing.

My guess is that he was a likeable fellow. He had a knack of making it easy for others to be kind to him. He was paralyzed, completely unable to get around on his own. Such a state of helplessness often produces a cranky character. It can turn an invalid into one extreme or the other: either a fussbudget, full of demands for service, or else a stubborn recluse, touchy about any acts of kindness that remind him of his state of need.

It seems that he was neither. He was the kind of patient that would be a favorite with nurses. He would have been docile, gentle, possibly humorous, easy to accommodate, easy to do favors for. He probably had a twinkle in his eye and a kind word for others, even when he was feeling miserable.

Those four friends of his were not just perfunctory paramedics. If they were, they would have gone right back home once they discovered there was no way to carry him into the house. "Well," they would have said, "we did our best. Nothing in our contract says we have to work overtime. Sorry, buddy. We'll just bring you back home and make you as comfortable as we can."

They did not do that. They loved their friend. This was a chance in a lifetime . . . and, traffic-jam or no traffic-jam, nothing was going to stop them from getting the man within the healing reach of Jesus.

Ingenuity went to work, stirred by love and the resolve never to say die. It must have been a hazardous adventure: physically hazardous, for they might have slipped; financially hazardous, for they might have had a law-suit on their hands because of damage done to private property. Such considerations did not matter. Nothing mattered except doing this favor for their friend.

The roof opened up, and down from the skies came this man in need of help. He was helped — more than anyone had counted on. He was healed of his physical disability and forgiven all his sins as well.

"Seeing their faith," Jesus was moved to drop whatever he was doing and immediately attend to them. Later in his ministry, Jesus said that we must "storm heaven" with our prayers and never give up. Perhaps he had the friends of the paralytic in mind. They certainly did just that — well, if not heaven, at least a replica of heaven in the shape of a thatched roof.

The whole scene contains many of the ingredients of Christmas. Indeed some commentators believe this to be St. Mark's version of the Christmas story. There was the opening of "the heavens." There was the sudden appearance of God's loving concern for humankind. There was proof of this concern in the visible form of mercy and healing. There was the shepherd-like astonishment expressed by all the bystanders. There were words of solemn praise that summed up the event in much the same way the angels responded to the Nativity: "Glory to God in the highest (rooftop) and peace (to the paralytic) on whom God's favor rests!"

Only in Mark's Gospel does Jesus call the man a child, without qualification. In Luke's account, Jesus refers to him as *friend*. Matthew says that Jesus called him child, but prefaced this diminutive with a word normally associated with grown-ups: "*Courage*, my child, your sins are forgiven." Only Mark develops this scene as a Christmas happening — as though a thoughtful father were giving a precious gift to his little one: "My child, your sins are forgiven . . . get up, pick up your stretcher, and go off home."

I like to think of the whole scene from this "Christmassy" point of view. Although he was an adult, the man seems to have retained that endearing quality that children have, especially at Christmas. He was able to receive things graciously and delightfully. He could accept help from his four friends, even when they risked his life as well as theirs. He was obviously able to do the same with Jesus. Our Lord's response was simple, straightforward, and accompanied by heartfelt joy.

The Scribes and Pharisees gave Jesus trouble. They were very difficult people for letting favors be done to them. Compulsively, they had to be on the giving end of all giving-receiving relationships. Initiative had to begin with them, even in their relationship with God. I'm sure that if they were paralytics, they wouldn't want friends to do them favors. That would have established a dependency of gratitude . . . and dependency of any kind is what proud people want to avoid at all costs.

Not so with "Master Christmas." That is why I gave him the name: "Master" instead of Mister, to suggest the child-like qualities of life he still enjoyed; "Christmas" because he demonstrated that most essential aspect of the Christmas spirit — the capacity to receive goodness, from others first, and then from God.

"The man got up, picked up his stretcher at once and walked out in front of everyone." As children show off their favorite Christmas gifts to the whole family, this man was delightfully displaying his new-found mobility. A happy mood came over the whole room: "All were astounded and praised God saying, 'We have never seen anything like this!'"

It never would have happened unless the man, admitting that he needed help, let himself be helped by four good friends. He then continued in the same spirit of amiable acceptance to let himself be helped by Jesus. Finally, he relished with spontaneous delight the lovely gift of wholeness he enjoyed.

To some extent, we all have this "spirit of Master Christmas" within us. We have it for the simple reason that we were all children once. Children are needy people, dependent on others for strength, force-fulness, and practical decisions about what to do when they are sick.

Children are like that paralytic who agreeably accepted help from his strong, forceful, practical friends. Children also take sheer delight in being given things. They don't play games like saying "You shouldn't have!" to a person who does them favors. They don't slink away from compliments with some brush-off phrase which is suppos-ed to indicate humility. They'll take all the affirmation they can get. They'll enjoy all the kindness, all the gifts, that come their way.

Grownups sometimes grow out of this ingenuous affability. It is very difficult to do favors for some people. Of course, there are some individuals — especially the handicapped and the aged — who have to struggle to assert their own need to be self-reliant. In order to stand up to those who want to over-help them, they must use whatever strength they have to keep from being weakened into abject dependency.

Also, it is not right, once childhood is over, to be always on the receiving end of other people's kindness. Such one-sided behavior is sick as well as selfish. There must be give, not only take, in all give-and-take relationships.

Even so, even after all is said about the need for healthy self-affir-mation and the necessity of active love, it is still true that most of us overdo it on the giving side of our adult relationship.

Most grownups, most of the time, react with embarrassment when they receive favors. Try complimenting them and they will push your words away. Say something genuinely affirming and they will change the subject. Give them a gift or pick up the check at a restaurant and they will either reject your generosity or make you feel uncomfortable by showing you how uncomfortable your gift has made them.

It is a delicate job to give well *and* to receive well. Whether giving advice, help, favors, or Christmas presents, there is need for tact and gentle consideration of the other person's need for assistance; we must balance that against his or her need for independence.

As difficult as it is to be a good giver, it is even more difficult to be a good receiver. Perhaps this is simply because we are not children any more. Because we have lived so long in the stage of reliance upon others, it sometimes feels like we are reverting to dependency again when we accept any offer of help. A balance must somehow be made between proud standoffishness and servile acceptance of everybody's handouts. Such a balance is not easy to manage. We have to learn from the mistakes we make by going to either extreme.

Jesus said we must be like little children in our agreeable acceptance of his grace. In our relationship with God, there is no give and take at all. We are completely on the receiving end; we receive created life from God, the fuller life we have in Christ, and the hope of afterlife — all from God. The only thing we can give back is our thanks and thoughtfulness.

Perhaps the best way to get in the right frame of mind for this kind of receivership is shown by the paralytic in the Gospel. Master Christmas teaches us the opposite of proud independence. He was happy about being helped by his friends. There were no cranky undertones, no grumbling touchiness, no gestures of querulous independence. He said yes to their impromptu plan for getting him to see the Great Physician.

Jesus praised the four stretcher-bearers; they made his work easy. All Jesus had to do was to help the man in the same way they did. It was a deeper, more thorough kind of help, but the same approach was used. They had already set up the mood for the miracle to happen.

Jesus didn't have to praise the man's faith; he only had to give him healing and forgiveness. The man was already open to such a possibility; like a child wide-eyed with Christmas, he was delightfully agreeable to grace.

Prayer of Master Christmas Within

Jesus, my Lord,
    help me to be your affable allowancer.

Let me have the spirit
    which the paralytic showed so comfortably.
He didn't mind the quick impulsiveness of his four friends;
    the rocking of the ropes as he was lifted up,
    then let down,
    the risk of life,
    the strain on his weakened limbs.
He let them help him their way.
He was responsive in his neediness,
    and joyful in the way he received their love.

He made it easy for you to love him larger —
    as you forgave his sins,
    showed your power over all paralysis,
    and watched him walking with new legs in front of everyone.

Let me be not-forgetful of my needs;
    not so all bent on self-reliance
    that I cannot respond gratefully
        to helps allowed,
        advice accepted,
        impromptu favors urged on me.
Let me relearn my childlike graciousness
    about the good things others do for me.

And from this learning to be open,
    let me give delight to you
    by waiting with ready welcome for your healing peace —
    your Christmas-given
    to my needs-received.

Amen.

17

(The Story of Us in Emmaus)

Emma and Cleopas

That very same day, two of [the disciples] were on their way to a village called Emmaus, seven miles from Jerusalem, and they were talking together about all that had happened. Now as they talked this over, Jesus himself came up and walked by their side; but something prevented them from recognizing him. He said to them, "What matters are you discussing as you walk along?" They stopped short, their faces downcast.

Then one of them, called Cleopas, answered him, "You must be the only person staying in Jerusalem who does not know the things that have been happening there these last few days." "What things?" he asked. "All about Jesus of Nazareth," they answered, "who proved he was a great prophet by the things he said and did in the sight of God and of the whole people; and how our chief priests and our leaders handed him over to be sentenced to death, and had him crucified. Our own hope had been that he would be the one to set Israel free. And this is not all: two whole days have gone by since it all happened..."

Then he said to them, "You foolish ones! So slow to believe the full message of the prophets! Was it not ordained that the Christ should suffer and so enter into his glory?" Then, starting with Moses and going through all the prophets, he explained to them the passages throughout the scriptures that were about himself.

When they drew near to the village to which they were going, he made as if to go on; but they pressed him to stay with them. "It is nearly evening," they said, "and the day is almost over."

137

So he went in to stay with them. Now while he was with them at table, he took the bread and said the blessing; then he broke it and handed it to them. And their eyes were opened and they recognized him; but he vanished from their sight. Then they said to each other, "Did not our hearts burn within us as he talked to us on the road and explained the scriptures to us?"

They set out that instant and returned to Jerusalem. There they found the Eleven assembled together with their companions, who said to them, "Yes, it is true. The Lord has risen and has appeared to Simon." Then they told their story of what had happened on the road and how they had recognized him at the breaking of the bread.

Luke 24:13-35

*E*very story in this book is about us, really. All the unnamed people in the Gospel — the good and not so good — can be recognized for what they are because we recognize their characteristics within ourselves.

But for the final story I want to be more deliberate, to put *us* right into the title, and only indirectly mention the two disciples who were making their slow, sad way to the village of Emmaus.

We know one of their names. St. Luke takes the trouble to say that "one of them, called Cleopas, said to Jesus..." The other person figures no less prominently in the story. It cannot be any of the Apostles; they were still in Jerusalem. It may not have been a man at all; women as well as men were followers of Jesus. Since the Evangelist's silence gives me liberty to think of the other disciple as I please, I am suggesting that it was a woman.

The name given her is completely arbitrary. I chose Emma simply because it is close to the sound of Emmaus. The desire to make her a woman is not arbitrary. I wanted to effect a balance, to give this story a sense of completeness.

I have the same purpose here that I had in the story of Minister Keep and Minister Going. In the case of these two disciples sent on their mission, it seemed right to think of one as an introvert and one as an extrovert, because every individual has something of these two ways of dealing with reality. Some people are more one way than the other, but all of us have both to a degree.

Likewise, when we consider male and female attributes, we all have both. A person who is "all masculine" would be an unsoftened, insufferable clod. A person who is "all feminine" would be an overly sensitive, indecisive jellyfish. But masculine and feminine characteristics brought together in an individual make for a well-rounded personality.

Therefore Cleopas and Emma, as representative man and woman, exist not only as "Us" — everybody alive today; they also exist as the "Us *within*" — the masculine and feminine traits that every person possesses, each to a different degree.

When Luke introduces the two disciples, they are people whose "faces were downcast." They were as low as low could be as they ran off to a town *they* had decided to go to, supporting one another in their mutual dejection, "talking together about all that had happened during the last few days."

The misery that contained them was so enveloping that they were prevented from recognizing Jesus. He was no more than a blur to them. He did not matter. Nothing mattered but their own grief, "as they walked along and looked sad."

Many other characters in this book had a story of sadness to tell. Each experienced different ways of feeling down. The Barley Boy had only a little bit to offer; the Canaanite woman suffered from unanswered prayers; the Gerasene Demoniac was pulverized by bitterness against himself and others; the lame man hated the way he was treated unfairly; the two disciples of Chapter 13 were dejected because people refused to receive their help.

There are many varieties of discouragement, each caused by a different situation. We make our own degree of identification with every one of them. Different temperaments can learn more from the personality of one story than from the next one. To the extent that the shoe fits, wear it.

The "Us in Emmaus," however, is altogether universal. The cause of this kind of sadness does not come from temperament or personality, or any kind of career development; it comes from our basic humanity. It is caused by the fundamental process of growth, which challenges all Christians simply because they are human.

The pair who walked seven miles to Emmaus were not dejected because some aspect of life let them down. Life *itself* let them down. Their depression was so all-inclusive, it is impossible to point out what was the cause of their condition.

They did specify the death of Jesus to the stranger they met: "Jesus
...proved he was a great prophet by the things he said and did in the
sight of God and of the whole people...and our leaders handed him
over...to be crucified." These were the facts, reported as one would
report the coming of a tornado. But the devastation resulting from
these facts was carried by the words: *our hopes have been shattered:*
"Our own hope was that he would be the one to set Israel free.
And...two whole days have gone by since it all happened."

Jesus told the disciples to meet him in Galilee after he rose from
the dead. They were going the other way, "faces downcast."

For three years, Jesus had served them as the focus of their understanding; he was the way by which they put meaning into their lives.
Expectations about who he was and what he would do was the
"glue" that made everything fit together.

Jesus was not the glue; *expectations*-about-Jesus was. They had
hoped that the great prophet of God would be the one to set Israel
free. He would be the one who would give value and security to their
lives. The two ideas were joined so tightly together; they could not
separate the Person from their own humanly constructed assump-
tions about the Person.

Consequently, when Jesus died, they became un-glued. Meaning
disappeared. Hopes turned to almost absolute depression.

It is the kind of depression that Kubler-Ross speaks about as the
last stage in the downhill slide of a dying patient (before integration
can take place). It is the kind of dark night described by St. John of
the Cross and all other experts of the spiritual life: darkness that
brings with it an overwhelming sense of powerlessness...when
things that used to matter don't matter any more...when people
and causes we cared about are listlessly abandoned...when lifestyles we knew as quite reasonable are no longer so. It is an experience that frustrates every shred of logic, every human hope for
meaning, every expectation of order and security.

There is only darkness. The two disciples speak of this experience
for us all: "We had hoped for _____; and now our hopes are
thwarted and life has gone out of us altogether!"

Jesus did not try to cheer them up. They were too disjointed for
any kind of optimistic "look on the bright side" counsel. Instead, he
criticized them very sternly: "You foolish ones! (The Greek word, in
this context, can also mean "You *burdens* who are wearing me
down!") You are so slow to believe the full message of the prophets."
This shocking statement should have made them feel even worse.
They were not only hopeless; they were dense as well! Somehow,

though, this new approach seemed to catch their interest in a way nothing else could.

The man who was still a stranger to them "explained all the passages of scripture (which showed how necessary it was) that the Christ should suffer and so enter into his glory." By means of history, our Lord developed a certain kind of logic. It was not the logic of natural sciences or mathematics or grammar or debate; it was the logic that spoke of what must happen if we are to grow. Christ's long history lesson may have referred to passages such as:

The grain of wheat must die in order to be more than just a grain of wheat (John 12:23).
A mother must go through the pain of childbirth before she has the joy of letting new life come into the world (John 16:20).
Because of suffering shall the one Just Servant reconcile all people to peace (Isaiah 53).
They that lose their lives will, in the losing, find a life more full than the one they lost (Matthew 16:24; Luke 9:23).

Suffering is also the one unarguable proof of love. Most likely, Jesus reminded the travelers about this part of his teaching, too:
When I am nailed up (on the Cross), I will draw all people to myself (John 3:14).
There is no greater proof of love than a man lay down his life for his friends (John 15:13).
I have come, not to be served, but to serve . . . This shall be a sign for you (Mark 10:40-45; Matthew 20:25-28; Luke 22:25-27; also Luke 2:12).

No one knows how long the discourse lasted. Perhaps Jesus met them halfway on their seven-mile journey. Doubtless, they were walking slowly and halted many times. It was a very spirited conversation. It might have taken an hour, maybe two.

"When they drew near to the village, Jesus made as if to go on." He will not force himself on anybody. They could freely invite him to deeper friendship, or they could let him go . . . regarding him as only a curious stranger one meets now and then on a long afternoon, someone who makes a little sense but leaves no lasting impression.

Jesus did not stand at the door and knock. He stood by the roadside, even started walking away, simply hoping to be invited in. They did so. At this point in the drama, the initiative was theirs, not his. "It is nearly evening," they said; and they urged him to dine with them.

They settled down to relax at a leisurely meal. Their minds, even their hearts could quiet down. They were not so full of their own devastating emptiness. They now let the stranger take the initiative. It wasn't just a good meal shared together. It was the Eucharist. Our Lord's words and gestures were the very same as at the Last Supper. This was the first Mass Jesus celebrated after Easter. "They recognized him at the breaking of the bread."

Our Lord was not only the explainer of God's logic, nourishing minds with new ways to handle hopelessness; he was also the nourisher of hearts, the personal gift of love.

The two disciples returned to Jerusalem. They related to the others how their hearts were on fire as Jesus explained things to them. But Christ's explanation not only calmed them down; it fed their intellects and gave them insights about suffering. Full recognition of Jesus, however, came only after Jesus was invited to be with them longer. The flame of love that fed their hearts did not reach them until Jesus said the blessing, broke the Bread, and gave of himself... himself.

When we are in deep trouble within ourselves, we have no trouble seeing *us* in the disciples of Emmaus. There have been times when we too have experienced our world caving in. We have become "unglued" in that thorough way described by spiritual writers as the "dark night." We *had hoped in* someone, or something... and we have felt overwhelming sadness when all our hopes collapsed.

In such a state, we are dealing, personally, with the problem of evil... one aspect of the problem of evil. We are also dealing with the problem of theology, for God and the meaning of our own lives are questioned. We murmur to others and to ourselves: "If God is good, why is there evil? Why must I suffer unjustly? Why should my baby have to die? Why are there cruel dictators, and hostage takers, and dope pushers? Why does a man 'who proved he was a great prophet by the things he said and did' have to be crucified and leave us floundering with downcast faces?" Why?

This is the problem of problems. It is the one that the human race has wrestled with since the world began. The ancient seers of Babylon and Egypt tried to solve it. The prophets of Israel — especially Jeremiah and Isaiah in his Suffering Servant passages — came closer than anyone to presenting the question correctly. Job embodied the problem; Jesus personified it and represented it. (Jesus did not solve it; he lived *through* it, loved *by* it, lived to explain that it must be.)

The problem is not yet solved. The Desert Fathers found it in a different context. Medieval people faced it in the plagues that devastated Europe. All people have to work it out for themselves when they meet wars, earthquakes, floods, or personal disasters.

No one is immune. Like the disciples on the road to Emmaus, we have wanted to be immune. We had hoped that the Christ — and, of course, ourselves — would not be forced to suffer. But it is not the way it is to be...

I will not presume to give a solution where such has never been found. I would like instead to offer a little homespun story with three episodes from ordinary life. They all concern two parents and their six-year-old son named Charlie. (Charlie is not necessarily representative. Not every child has gone through his particular trauma. He is just a boy — myself — whom I happen to remember.)

First episode: It is July. Charlie wakes up crying in the middle of the night. He has appendicitis. This is a great evil. Parents did not cause, do not wish, this suffering. They rush him to the hospital and wait out the crisis with worry and with prayers. They bless the doctor who operated successfully. All is well.

Second episode: Charlie heals. It is now August. Parents are watching out the window as their son plays in the sandbox with a boy his own age. Charlie is teasing him, aggravating him, throwing sand in his face. The boy retaliates with a well-timed sock in the nose. Charlie starts crying. His parents did not cause this evil thing called a bloody nose. But they allow it to happen. They certainly did less about it than the "July evil." They let Charlie learn, the hard way, how to relate with his peers.

Third episode: It is now September. Parents do a strange thing. They *cause* evil to happen to their son. They don't rush in to heal their boy, as they did in July (as Jesus did when he rescued the lame, the deaf, the blind, the possessed, the dead); they don't reluctantly *permit* the evil, as they did in August (as Jesus did when he wanted so much to love the people of Jerusalem, but simply wept for them because he could not interfere with their free will). This time the parents actually *cause* their boy to suffer. As for Charlie, this evil is worse than appendicitis and bloody nose put together. He is sent to school. The world he knew caves in during that first week of September. He had gotten used to one way of coping with reality. He was accustomed to being "king of the castle." There were few surprises and much security. He liked it that way; he expected things to stay the same.

Now he is pushed into a world of great surprises and little security.

He has to vie with many children for the attention of just one adult. He has to get used to new surroundings and new friends. He has to learn dull things like writing and reading and arithmetic. He had "hoped it would be otherwise . . . but it was not so."

Of course, we know that the parents caused the "September evil" because they loved their son. They loved him in their causing him to suffer as much as they loved him when they rushed him to the hospital so that he *wouldn't* suffer. Painful as it was, Charlie had to be put through the process of growth development.

The parents understood it. The child didn't . . . yet. He could only feel the pain of separation. He had to endure the pain longer before new integration could take place.

It is easy to see the difference in the case of Charlie. We are looking at the three incidents from the perspective of his parents. It is not so easy when the roles change, when God is the parent and we are the child.

Some suffering in the world is like the "July evil." God is against it. He sent his Son to be the Great Physician of our souls *and* bodies. He endorses all our efforts in the fields of healing, medicine, and social justice.

Some of our suffering is like the "August evil." God does not like dope pushers or dictators or drunken drivers who kill the innocent or anyone who sins against the neighbor. God sternly *dislikes* them and he will judge them at the end of time. But he cannot turn into stone every culprit who dares to inflict harm. If he did, he would have to take back the gift of free will. We would be no more than brute beasts, every one of us. We would be unable to love God or anyone. If we were all rendered incapable of inflicting evil, we would all likewise be unable to be responsible for the good we do. We would have no ability to make a choice.

There is also the third category of suffering. It is suggested by my analogy of Charlie being sent to school. It is the kind Jesus spoke of when he declared, "I must go through it, in order to enter into my glory." It is letting ourselves die to one life so that we may attain a fuller life, one which is possible only when the previous lifestyle is surrendered.

But surrendering involves sundering. This experience is never pleasant. We do not easily let go. Even infants at the very beginning of their lives experience pain before anything else. The first thing they do is cry. They are more aware of "dying" than of "being born." They were used to nine months of peaceful existence in their mother's womb. Then came the shattering experience of entering into new life. Fear, discomfort, and insecurity were their "commencement exercises." It was an unwelcome ushering.

There are many other ways life can be shattered. They are discussed in any number of books; they are experienced in a variety of ways. We feel them when we go through certain critical passages of life, such as the transplanting from grade school to high school, then from school responsibilities to adult responsibilities. Moving to a new location or entering a new career can jolt our system. We can become "unglued" when we notice vitality fade or are told to slow down. We can feel annihilated when those great dreams about ourselves or others turn out to be mere unfulfillable wishes. We certainly know the bite of anguish when at last we face the fact that we must die.

All of these — especially the last — causes great grief of soul. Like the disciples enroute to Emmaus, we become so dejected that all possibilities for life are blurred out. We can confuse "September evil" for "July evil," deciding that God has conclusively let us down, and we refuse to admit that he *may* simply be sending us off to another school of growth. During such times the sense of abandonment may possess us completely; the words of the Gospel may come back to haunt us: "We had hoped to be immune from sorrow . . . and it is not so."

Even for people who have loved Jesus all their lives, he can become a stranger during the darkness that grief brings. He usually does seem blurred whenever we feel dead to our own lives and forsaken of all our hopes. Even so, it is still a good idea to let him — *as stranger* — take us to the message of the Scriptures. There we can see the large designs of God's saving plan, how all the prophets showed that Christ and his friends must suffer in order to enter into glory.

We may encounter other strangers, too, who will help us understand the history of "September evil." Wise men and women of all ages, of every faith, have shown that *some* suffering is the proof of love; it is the only way to change from stagnant half-existence to a more integrated life.

These explanations can arrest our despondency to some extent. They can broaden the horizons of our thinking. They can sustain us, for a while, with new ways of accepting challenges to grow.

But, for all the books we read, all the workshops on self-actualization we attend, all the Scriptures we study — all these manifold explanations will be no more than a curious afternoon enjoyed with a stranger if we do not let the heart be nourished.

In some way, we have to do what Emma and Cleopas did. Initiative is ours. Jesus will not force his welcome. If we are to accept suffering in a way that will heal us into new wholeness, we have to invite Jesus to "stay with us" (even before we fully recognize him for all that he truly is). We have to relax with him, in leisure and in a spirit of prayer.

Things will be different once we ask him to remain. We will let him bless God for us; we will recognize him in the breaking of the bread; we will be nourished by the food of himself; we will be sustained in such a way that suffering becomes an essential part of our entering into Easter.

Jesus will not praise us as he did so many people before his resurrection; he will not have to. He becomes one with us in Holy Communion, by which he makes us whole. Our hearts will be burning with his love; our minds will be filled with his attitudes and explanations.

Jesus will not praise us; we will praise *him*. We will know him to be with us as we worship God our Father rightly... and as we return to those we love, "telling the story of what happened on our journey and how we had recognized him at the breaking of the bread."

Prayer of Emma and Cleopas Within

Jesus, my Lord,
    have mercy on me, a sinner.
Be patient with me when I have sad looks,
    when I lack hope,
    and go off on my own dejectedly.
I don't mean to feel so blown apart;
I don't really want to be so depressed...
    but I was hoping evil would not touch me
    (that is, certain kinds of evil —
    the ones I'm least equipped to cope with).
I was hoping love could be proved in some way
    other than by suffering.
I was expecting, once I reached adulthood
    that I wouldn't have to go through growing pains again.
    but I do have to,
    and I don't always like it.

I want to hold on to the life I know:
        the sureties of normal expectations,
        the learned routines of thought and action,
        which gave me meaning
                until I felt them die.
And then I journeyed to Emmaus, sadly:
        my world caved in,
        my hopes all gone,
        my willingness to live aborted.

I'm not sure those disciples of your Gospel
        were man and woman.
But I'm sure I have both in me:
I am both strong and sensitive;
        impulsive and intuitive.
Each aspect of me needs your visitation.
For strong can strongly want to quit
        when strength is powerless;
        and sensitivity can simply stagnate
        when nothing freshens heart with hope.

My Lord,
        my sometimes-Stranger,
        be kind enough to draw me back to history:
        explaining, once again,
        the lesson-plan of love,
        and the suffering that must be part of it.

Walk slowly, as you seem to leave me,
        so that I can invite you to stay longer
        in the more leisured atmosphere of prayer....

Give me the blessing of your holy Mass,
        the breaking of your Bread of Life,
        so that I can then recognize you fully
        and burn with new desire to live,
        to serve,
        and be with you forever:
        world without suffering,
        world without end.

Amen.

Appendix

Some Further Ideas
On the Introjective Method of This Book

There has been a considerable use of the word *within* throughout these chapters. A constant contention has been that "there is a bit of the Barley Boy (and Company) in us all.

It might seem to suggest that a very crowded personality is contained in every individual. The seventeen chapters focused on twenty or so heroes. Added to these were a few other unheroic individuals (like the old grouch of St. John's Gospel, Chapter 8) who, it was assumed, reflected certain unwholesome aspects of our behavior. Also, there were some groups (the Pharisees and the Apostles) who collectively displayed certain character traits which we at times, can confess to be our own.

All told, there are many different people claiming a piece of "soul territory" within the personality of every Christian alive today. Some explanation seems to be in order.

The procedure throughout this book has been the "projection technique" in reverse. Everyone by now knows the psychological device called projection. There are two sides of it, negative and positive.

Negative projection has been worked over more thoroughly than positive, ever since Freud. This trick we play on ourselves goes something like this: First: We are subconsciously uncomfortable about certain attitudes or desires within us; we are not fully aware of these drives, but we do have a dimly-discerned unrest about them. Second: Not wanting to admit such things to ourselves (we would rather they were entirely foreign to us), we project them on to other people, pinning on them the qualities that we can't live with. Third: Once this "throwing up and onto somebody else" is done, we feel better about ourselves and we feel justified in hating, or fearing, the person who has gotten stuck with our projections. Bigotry, snobbery, race prejudices, genocide, character assassination — all these evils proceed from negative projections.

Positive projection is just as deceptive, and often just as pernicious. We have some *good* sides of our personality that we are unwilling to own up to consciously. There are different reasons for such unwillingness. We can be lazy: if we really took possession of our goodness, we would also have to take responsibility for the qualities that make us good. Such responsibility demands work on our part: to keep developing and improving these qualities. We don't want to work at this, sometimes. So we "forget" that we have them.

Also, we can be victims of double messages coming from remembered childhood. One message can still be trying to deny the other. Certain instincts, based on honest feedback from friends, tell us we are lovable and capable; we are worthwhile in the areas of *being* and *doing*. Yet, for some of us, early training set up such high standards or regimented us with so many stern reproofs that we became convinced of just the opposite: we could not be loved, could not be trusted to do anything right. Consequently, if we now admit we are really worthwhile, we would defy those mighty indictments from parents, teachers, and peers when they put us in our place. Such defiance is risky. So we deny ourselves rather than change the image.

We often push our goodness underground this way, refusing to admit that we are all of what we are. We "repress the sublime."*

It is a quick step, then, to start projecting (positively). We attribute to others all those enviable qualities we have hidden from ourselves. We fall helplessly and irrationally in love. We give ourselves heart and soul to an impressive personality like the leader of a gang or to a dictator like Rev. Jimmie Jones or Adolf Hitler. We become such fanatics of a football team or a popular singer that we either sell our souls for a ticket to the game or risk being crushed to death by a frenzied mob. We make a god of someone who seems to have what we're convinced we lack so desperately. *(The Denial of Death,* by Ernest Becker, 1974, is a very good description of this phenomenon.)

Not all projection is bad, of course. If we had no capacity for throwing ourselves out to others, there would be no compassion, no understanding of what makes other people tick, no language, no bridges at all between one individual and another.

With all the good it does, however, it is a troublesome way of operating when projection amounts to disowning what rightfully belongs to us.

The method of this book is to suggest that we take back what was ours in the first place, both the good and the bad qualities. This could be called the subjective, or "introjective," approach. It takes what seems to be on the outside and turns what is out there back into oneself. It performs the same function inwardly that a mirror does to our superficial appearance. That is why I used that analogy in my introduction.

The method is not a new one. Psychologists, especially those influenced by Jung, have been applying this method for years. One way to appreciate the significance of dreams, for instance, is to understand every aspect of the dream as a projection of some part of self. All the various details remembered — whether it's Uncle Jim, or a sharp knife, or a strange building, or a sled called Rosebud — can be seen as part of me. They are simply the raw material used by the unconscious in order to warn or praise or somehow instruct the conscious mind. The work of interpretation, then, is to "introject" the material after I reflect on "What part of me do I see in the person I know as Uncle Jim?"; "What is signified to me by a sharp knife?"; "What do I feel when I see a strange building like that?"; "What associations are brought up when I remember my childhood sled?"

When such objects are thought about as "parts of me" trying to tell me something, the dream can often make more sense than it can by trying to take in the meaning at its objective face value.

Such a procedure goes farther back than modern psychology. Jung himself admits his indebtedness to the early Fathers of the Church. In *The Interpretation of Visions* (Vol. I, Page 102), Jung refers to the Sheep and Goats Parable (Matthew's Gospel, Chapter 25) in which Jesus promises eternal happiness to those who have cared for "the least of my brethren": "I was hungry, thirsty, in prison, a stranger, etc. and you cared... Since you have cared for the least of my brethren, I consider it to have been done for me."

Some of the Church Fathers understood this passage to apply *primarily* to oneself. Jung states, "Already in the first century after Christ there were philosophers who held that the least of one's brethren, the inferior man, is oneself; they therefore directly read [this passage] on the subjective level."*

* The starting place for much of this has come from *Ego and Archetype,* by Edward F. Edinger, Penguin Books, 1972. For a further development of "The least of my brethren = me" see pages 136-138 and 142-146.

One further illustration comes from the Sermon on the Mount (Matthew 5:23-24). Jesus makes a statement that sounds like an unequivocal command. It is a command, however, that is almost impossible to obey. It has probably caused Christians more difficulties — almost despair — than any other passage. The words are:

"If you are bringing your offering to the altar
and there remember
that your brother (read: 'anyone')
has *something against you,*
leave your offering there before the altar,
go and be reconciled with your brother first,
and then come back and present your offering."

The obvious implication is that if you do *not* obtain a reconciliation, your prayers and worshipful presence at the altar won't do you any good. God will turn his back on you because your gift is unworthy.

Note the emphasized phrase *"if you remember that your brother has anything against you."* It points out the impossibility of Christ's command if it is understood objectively. If such is the case, Jesus himself did not follow his own injunction. King Herod had *something against* our Lord. He wanted the prophet of Galilee to play the fool and perform a few flashy miracles. The only way Jesus could be reconciled to that unsufferable monarch was to deny his own mission and significance. Jesus did not do so. He did not say a word. There was no reconciliation (Luke 23:8-12).

Judas had *something against* him. Our Lord simply and sadly let him go.

The Scribes and Pharisees (all but a few of them) had *something against* Jesus, even to the point of calling for his crucifixion. Jesus was never able to be reconciled to them. He tried, but he didn't manage it. They demanded that Jesus become someone they would find more suitable, someone they could control. Jesus could not submit to their stipulations and no reconciliation was effected. Yet, this did not mean Christ's offering on the altar of the cross was displeasing to God his Father.

As with Christ, so with the Christian. There are people whom we just cannot be reconciled to. Some are so embittered against us, we cannot befriend them no matter what we do. Some lay down so many conditions that to agree to reconciliation on their terms would be tantamount to self-surrender. How can a woman be reconciled to a rapist? How can a man or woman be reconciled to a person who demands abject submission to *every* whim as a prerequisite for acceptance?

We must, of course, forgive anyone toward whom we harbor a grudge. This is within our power. We must also ask forgiveness and seek to negotiate a peace with anyone who harbors a grudge against us. But sometimes it is impossible.

How can we understand Christ's words rightly? He does not say: "Those whom *we* have offended" or "Those whom *we* have something against;" he says: "Those who have something against *us*."

We can obey Christ's commandment literally only when we consider it from the subjective point of view. Some of the early Church Fathers considered it so: "If you bring your gift to the altar, and there remember that you have anything against *yourself,* leave then your gift and first be reconciled to *yourself* and then come and offer your gift."

Understood this way, Christ's statement makes perfect sense. Once we interpret the command to be the work of reconciliation with self, there are no excusing clauses, no extenuating circumstances.

Sin is one way that we "do something against ourselves" as well as against God and others. We must be reconciled not only by asking forgiveness from God and those we have harmed; we must also be reconciled to that selfish side of us that did the sinning. We must let God's forgiveness grace us with the power to forgive ourselves. If we don't, we are still living a double life, with part of us still left unbefriended by the rest of us. We cannot offer our whole self to God as long as we are still bitter against ourselves for having done such stupid or sinful things.

Besides sin, there can be certain aspects of our personality that we have either deliberately submerged or else allowed to atrophy by inattentiveness. For instance, an over-controlled individual may squelch his sensitive or playful nature; a playboy may stifle his serious side; an intuitive person may forsake the world of reality in order to feed his dreams; a pragmatic person may refuse all truth except that which can be tested by the five senses.

Examples could go on and on. These are enough to show that sometimes we have not grown in all the ways that God wants us to. There are parts of us underdeveloped. We have been slipshod in certain areas of our make-up. These areas could be considered "characters within ourselves" which object to being relegated to the limbo of non-expression. As such, they "have something against us." We must be reconciled to them. We must find ways to let them come alive in us and grow as much as they can.

When this happens, we can more genuinely approach the altar. "All of us" will bring the offering — in concert, in harmony, with no parts at odds against the rest of us, with all our qualities working effectively and peacefully.

It's not that we have to be perfect in developing all sides of our per-

sonality before God will accept us. All that is needed is to be open to
further growth, to not deliberately stunt any part of ourselves, which
God and others have a right to expect.

Such were the theological considerations and psychological prem-
ises which formed the background for the procedure of this book. I
used the method of *projection in reverse* as some early Christian
writers did with certain statements of Jesus and as some modern
gestalt schools do in their analysis of dreams.

My contention has been that we can look at certain famous and
not so famous people of the Gospels and understand them to be the
"raw material" for appreciating our own personal relationship to
Jesus. We can draw from their characteristic qualities and make
them our own. By doing so, we can possess these qualities even
more thoroughly than we already have. We can be reconciled to
more parts of our amazingly complex selves. We can then be better
students of Christ's instructions, better receptors of his challenges
and praise.

The unnamed people of this book have done it for me. I hope they
have done it for you as well.

also by Father Powers

Quiet Places with Jesus

40 Guided Imagery Meditations for Personal Prayer

This book sets forth the dynamic personal prayer method called "guided imagery meditation." It is the same method Father Powers uses during his retreats for Christians of many lifestyles. The meditation process infuses a new confidence in adults' ability to pray and enjoy a spiritually rewarding life.

Guided Imagery cuts through busy schedules, harried nerves and daily distractions and taps the hidden power of our memories and imaginations to influence thought patterns. This method releases the Spirit within us, lifts our minds to a "quiet place," and turns our hearts to God.

Quiet Places with Jesus offers 40 such guided meditations. Each begins with a Scripture quotation followed by a reflection and then the actual step-by-step meditative method. Topics focus on all those areas most important to us – discouragement, anger, others' opinions of us, self-awareness, rejection, love, and so on.

Three appendixes (1) provide additional material on prayer and meditation, (2) correlate specific problems with appropriate meditations and (3) arrange meditations specifically for lenten use.

Available from your local bookseller or
Twenty-Third Publications, P.O. Box 180,
Mystic, CT 06355 1-203-536-2611

also by Father Powers

Daily Scripture Meditations for Lent

Father Powers' *40 Scripture Meditations for Lent* follows the tradition of his other prayer books–giving the Christian a chance to encounter and embrace the Lord.

For each day in Lent, teens and adults find here a short gospel selection, a prayer, and a suggested lenten practice. For a few minutes in the morning, on the way to work or school, during a daily church visit, or after lenten worship services, this prayerbook has the power to help you make the most out of Lent.

Available from your local bookseller or
Twenty-Third Publications, P.O. Box 180,
Mystic, CT 06355   1-203-536-2611

also by Father Powers

Advent Prayers
and
Scripture Meditations

The days of Advent have long been passed by as opportunities for spiritual nourishment for adults and teens. This need no longer be the case.

Father Powers has again turned his retreat experience into a practical seasonal guide for faith and prayer from which every committed adult and teen can derive pleasure and benefit.

The easy-to-use daily format nurtures the reader with a gospel reflection, an Advent blessing prayer, and a personal prayer that can be said on its own or in conjunction with the lighting of the candles on an Advent wreath.

The book culminates with household and family prayers appropriate for the Christmas season.

Available from your local bookseller or
Twenty-Third Publications, P.O. Box 180,
Mystic, CT 06355   1-203-536-2611